What Works! Successful Strategies for Pursuing National Board Certification Version 3.1

What Works! Successful Strategies for Pursuing National Board Certification Version 3.1

Components 3 and 4

Second Edition

Bobbie Faulkner

BLOOMSBURY ACADEMIC
NEW YORK • LONDON • OXFORD • NEW DELHI • SYDNEY

BLOOMSBURY ACADEMIC

Bloomsbury Publishing Inc, 1359 Broadway, New York, NY 10018, USA
Bloomsbury Publishing Plc, 50 Bedford Square, London, WC1B 3DP, UK
Bloomsbury Publishing Ireland, 29 Earlsfort Terrace, Dublin 2, D02 AY28, Ireland

BLOOMSBURY, BLOOMSBURY ACADEMIC and the Diana logo are trademarks of Bloomsbury Publishing Plc

First published in the United States of America 2026

Copyright © Bloomsbury Publishing Inc, 2026

Cover image: © istock/5second

All rights reserved. No part of this publication may be: i) reproduced or transmitted in any form, electronic or mechanical, including photocopying, recording or by means of any information storage or retrieval system without prior permission in writing from the publishers; or ii) used or reproduced in any way for the training, development or operation of artificial intelligence (AI) technologies, including generative AI technologies. The rights holders expressly reserve this publication from the text and data mining exception as per Article 4(3) of the Digital Single Market Directive (EU) 2019/790.

Bloomsbury Publishing Inc does not have any control over, or responsibility for, any third-party websites referred to or in this book. All internet addresses given in this book were correct at the time of going to press. The author and publisher regret any inconvenience caused if addresses have changed or sites have ceased to exist, but can accept no responsibility for any such changes.

A catalog record for this book is available from the Library of Congress

ISBN: HB: 9781475875195
PBK: 9781475875201
ePDF: 9781475875218
eBook: 9798765164914

Typeset by Deanta Global Publishing Services, Chennai, India
Printed and bound in the United States of America

For product safety related questions contact productsafety@bloomsbury.com.

To find out more about our authors and books visit www.bloomsbury.com and sign up for our newsletters.

Contents

Preface vi

Introduction 1

1 What Is National Board Certification? 3

2 Building Your Foundation 7

3 Getting Started and Getting Support 13

4 Writing for the National Board 21

5 Component 3: Teaching Practice and Learning Environment: The Video Component 37

6 Component 4: Effective and Reflective Practitioner 65

7 Scoring 89

8 Confusing Terms, Topics, and FAQs 93

9 Candidate Care 99

Appendix A: Ten Commandments for Survival as a National Board Candidate 107
Appendix B: Ten Editing Tips to Trim Space without Trimming Content 109
Appendix C: Sentence Stems for Analytic and Reflective Writing 110
Appendix D: Component 3: Analysis of a Video 111
Appendix E: Video Tips for Component 3 112
Appendix F: SSTARS Lesson Plan Template Based on the Architecture of Accomplished Teaching 114
Appendix G: Twenty Tips from Component 4 Assessors 116
About the Author 118

Preface

This book is written to support candidates doing Components 3 and/or 4 of the current Version 3.1 of the National Board Certification process. While the content of Components 3 and 4 hasn't changed since its final roll-out in 2016, National Board Certified Teachers (NBCTs) have gained knowledge and experience useful to candidates pursuing certification. This volume reflects such collective knowledge.

Introduction

The *What Works!* book series for National Board candidates began with an off-the-cuff remark. "You ought to write a book," a fellow Candidate Support Provider (CSP) said one day after a workshop for candidates. So that's what I did. This publication is actually the fifth in the *What Works!* series, and the second to address the revised 3.0 version.

What Works! Successful Strategies for Pursuing National Board Certification Version 3.1, Components 3 and 4 joins it's companion book about Components 1 and 2, and replaces all earlier versions of the series.

What Works! Successful Strategies for Pursuing National Board Certification Version 3.1, Components 3 and 4 is not endorsed by the NBPTS or any other involved in the National Board Certification process. It's not meant to be a "Cliff Notes" type of publication one can use to circumvent the NBPTS documents and instructions.

What Works! Successful Strategies for Pursuing National Board Certification Version 3.1, Components 3 and 4 contains tips, opinions, information, documents, and examples that have been created solely for the purposes of demonstration and are neither approved nor endorsed by the NBPTS: Keep in mind that:

- The author is not a trained assessor and does not imply that any sample writing would score well and/or lead to certification according to the NBPTS Scoring Rubrics.
- All samples are hypothetical, fabricated, made up, and are not from actual candidate writing. They cannot be copied for use within a component.
- *What Works! Successful Strategies for Pursuing National Board Certification, Version 3.1, Components 3 and 4* is as current as I can make it. However, it is the responsibility of the candidate to be fully informed of the current NBPTS requirements in case directions change after the book's publication.

This update is a labor of love for my fellow educators and National Board candidates. It is my hope that the information will make your journey toward National Board Certification just a little easier, more meaningful, and successful.

1 What Is National Board Certification?

Six Word Memoir: Know your standards. Know them well!
BRITNEY, NC

NBPTS Background and History

National Board Certification is a national *voluntary* system that certifies teachers who meet a set of high and rigorous standards for what accomplished teachers should know and be able to do. This certification system was developed by the National Board for Professional Teaching Standards (NBPTS) and put in place in 1987 following recommendations from the Carnegie reports *A Nation at Risk* and *A Nation Prepared*.

The National Board has developed high, rigorous, research-based standards to measure the effectiveness of a teacher's practice. Teachers complete a series of written exercises that probe the depth of their knowledge of their subject matter. The process involves an extensive series of performance-based assessments that include:

- Teaching portfolios.
- Student work samples.
- Written commentaries.
- Videos.
- Analysis of the teacher's classroom practice and the impact on student learning.

The work is based on long-established research that identifies and recognizes sound educational practices that result in student learning. The NBPTS has commissioned more than 140 studies and papers on the value of the certification process as well as its standards and assessment. The process has also been validated by a number of independent studies.

The Five Core Propositions

The Core Propositions are the heart of the National Board process. They outline the expectations and values for what *accomplished* teachers should know and be able to do, and are the umbrella under which the other elements of the National Board Certification process are organized. Accomplished teaching implies going *above and beyond* what is typically expected of the average teacher. The Propositions describe skills in the following areas:

Proposition 1: Commitment to Students

- Accomplished teachers know the developmental levels of their students, believe that all students can learn regardless of background, and use their knowledge to design effective instruction for all students and a variety of learning styles.

Proposition 2: Knowledge of Subject

- Building upon their knowledge of students, accomplished teachers advance their own understanding of their content area and develop a wide range of strategies to set high and worthwhile goals to teach that subject matter to their students.

Proposition 3: Manage and Monitor Student Learning

- Accomplished teachers understand how to manage, motivate, monitor, and assess student learning by planning appropriate learning sequences to achieve the desired outcomes and adjusting instruction as needed. Accomplished teachers also know how to structure the learning environment for optimum learning.

Proposition 4: Think Systematically about Their Teaching and Learn from Experience

- Accomplished teachers analyze student learning and reflect on their teaching practice. They then determine the next set of high and worthwhile goals, implement appropriate instruction, and continue the analysis and reflection cycle.

Proposition 5: Teachers Are Members of Learning Communities

- Accomplished teachers collaborate with other professionals, parents, and their larger community to support and enhance student learning.

The National Board Standards

There are twenty-five certificates that cover many subject areas and student development levels. Each contains a set of Standards, which, along with the Five Core Propositions, form the foundation of National Board Certification. The Standards identify specific knowledge, skills, and attitudes that support accomplished practice while emphasizing the holistic nature of teaching. They identify how a teacher's professional judgment is reflected in action and they reflect the Five Core Propositions. They identify what an accomplished teacher should know and be able to do.

To achieve National Board Certification and be considered an accomplished teacher, a candidate must show *clear, convincing, and consistent evidence that his or her teaching practice reflects the Standards*. Understanding the standards and how to demonstrate them in practice provides evidence of accomplished teaching.

WHAT WORKS! Understanding Your Standards

- *Read* the standards multiple times. Pay attention to the examples included in each.
- *Think* about how you already incorporate the standards in your teaching.
- *Highlight* things you already do regularly in one color, things you do sometimes in a second color, and things you rarely or never do in a third color. This will help you recognize your strengths and which areas might be bolstered in your practice.
- *Show* clear, consistent, convincing evidence that your teaching is based on the National Board Standards.

WHY IT WORKS! The standards were developed to identify accomplished teaching. Candidates are expected to show evidence of the standards within their teaching.

The Process

National Board Certification is a rigorous process that may take up to five years to achieve. Candidates are asked to:

- *Demonstrate* within their teaching practice the rigorous standards discussed above.
- *Show* leadership, collaboration, learning, reflective practice, and professionalism.
- *Prepare* a portfolio of three (3) written entries that document their teaching practice.
- *Focus* on the analysis of student work samples, classroom practice and professional development, collaboration, and leadership.
- *Make* videos of the teacher working with his/her class.
- *Complete* a series of subject-specific computer tests at an Assessment Center to document knowledge of their content area.

National Board Certification is the highest, most comprehensive voluntary professional development experience available to teachers. Examining their teaching practices and professional accomplishments in depth provides teachers a professional growth experience unlike any other.

2 Building Your Foundation

You know you are a National Board Candidate when your idea of summer reading is poring over grade level teaching manuals for the Assessment Center instead of enjoying juicy romance novels.
ROSEMARY

Who Is an Accomplished Teacher?

In a nutshell, an accomplished teacher is one who goes *above and beyond* what is typically expected. Accomplished teachers practice exceptional, skilled teaching. They have a strong knowledge base of subject matter and pedagogy, demonstrate complex, nuanced professional work, and consistently meet rigorous standards of practice. Above all, accomplished teachers are committed to their students, know their subjects and how to teach them, know how to manage and monitor student learning, reflect on their practice and learn from their experience, and are learners, collaborators, and leaders within their professional communities.

Accomplished teachers are teachers just like you, who try their best every day to meet their students' needs, keep current with pedagogy and subject knowledge, and work with others in their schools and districts to create an environment conducive to supporting the healthy growth and development of their students academically, socially, and emotionally.

What Is Accomplished Teaching?

Accomplished teaching is the entwined double helix of knowing your subject and how to teach it, as shown in the Architecture of Accomplished Teaching graphic discussed in the the General Portfolio document and found on the National Board website, Candidate Resources page. The two strands are closely interwoven and almost seamlessly connected. Accomplished teaching combines both the art and craft of teaching along with a solid knowledge base of content and child development.

Accomplished teaching means planning and demonstrating effective instruction for *these students, at this time, in this place*. The National Board describes accomplished teaching practices in the Standards developed for each certificate. They are the specific teaching behaviors that accomplished teachers demonstrate within their teaching practice. As a candidate for National Board Certification, you need to show evidence of the standards in your teaching practice.

The Architecture of Accomplished Teaching

The Architecture of Accomplished Teaching (AAT) is the National Board version of an accomplished lesson/unit plan. It's a double helix representation of accomplished teaching practice as it applies to the lessons candidates use in their entries and in assessment center exercises. It is designed to give a visual representation of how the accomplished teaching of units of study and lessons is organized. It is an under-used tool that can add greatly to the understanding of the National Board process and what the National Board is "looking for." You can find it in the GENERAL Portfolio Instructions document and in the "What Teachers Should Know and Do" booklet found in the HOMEROOM section of the NB website. Many prompts you'll respond to in your Written Commentaries are connected to specific steps on the AAT.

Candidates often lament that if they just knew what the National Board "wanted," they'd know what to do for each component. In truth, candidates who understand the Architecture of Accomplished Teaching and use its structure as the basis for planning their lesson sequences will demonstrate what the assessors want—evidence of accomplished teaching. I suggest posting a copy of it near your computer for frequent and easy reference. See the AAT in the Appendix.

What Works! Studying the Architecture of Accomplished Teaching

Read the Architecture of Accomplished Teaching from the bottom up.

Step 1 - Start with knowledge of your students. *(Proposition 1)*

- Who are they? Where are they now in their learning? Where should you begin?
- What knowledge about your students influenced the goals you set?

- How do you incorporate this knowledge into your lesson planning?
- What will success for your students look like?

Step 2 - Continue setting high, worthwhile goals. *(Proposition 1)*

- How do the goals you set connect to your standards and portfolio instructions?
- How do the goals fit into the sequence of your overarching goals?
- What do you want your students to know by the end of the lesson or unit?

Step 3 - Implement Instruction. *(Proposition 2)*

- What approaches/strategies do you plan to use to accomplish your goals?
- In what sequence might you plan the strategies you plan to use?
- How will the strategies you choose support your students' learning?
- What is your rationale for implementing instruction this way?
- What criteria might you use to decide if and when to use another strategy?

Step 4 - Evaluate Student Learning. *(Proposition 3)*

- How will you assess student learning?
- Why did you choose these methods for these students at this time, in this setting?
- What evidence will let you know that the instruction was successful—or not?
- What, if anything, did the assessment(s) tell you about your instruction?
- Where will you go next?

Step 5 - Reflect on the effectiveness of your lesson design and decisions. *(Proposition 4)*

- How do you know whether you made the right choices?
- What was successful and what was not?
- How could students reflect on their own learning?

Step 6 - Set new, high, worthwhile goals. *(Proposition 4)*

- How will you decide when it is time to move on in the lesson sequence?
- What indicators will you use to set new goals?

SSTARS: Here is an acronym to jog your memory.

- **S**tudents: Know your students and how they learn. Proposition 1
- **S**et high, worthwhile, and appropriate goals. Propositions 1 and 2
- **T**each using appropriate, effective strategies. Propositions 2 and 3
- **A**ssess student progress using a variety of evaluation types and forms. Proposition 3
- **R**eflect on your teaching and your students' progress. Proposition 4
- **S**tart the process again.

See Appendix for a lesson plan template that uses SSTARS. Revisit the Architecture of Accomplished Teaching in Chapter 9.

Why It Works!

The elements of the Architecture of Accomplished Teaching provide a complete lesson/unit plan that will have the greatest impact on student learning.

What Works! Knowing When to Use the Writing Styles.

- Use mainly *descriptive* writing with some analysis for Steps 1, 2, and 3.
- Use mainly *analytical* writing for Step 4.
- Use mainly *analytical and reflective* writing for Steps 5 and 6.

Why It Works!

Use the Architecture of Accomplished Teaching to discern the nuances in the prompt. This will help you use the appropriate writing style for each. The prompts align with the Architecture's steps and using it will help you find evidence of your thinking and teaching to write about.

The Scoring Guide

The Scoring is an underutilized resource that can be a life-saver. The assessors use them as they score your work. How your component will be scored is not a secret! Everything you need to show evidence of is listed in bullet format in the Scoring Rubrics.

What Works! Including the 3-Cs of Evidence:
- *Clear:* Anyone who reads your written commentary should be able to understand what you are saying. You've explained acronyms and educational terms. The sequence of events can be easily followed. Your writing is readable and makes sense.
- *Consistent:* Your writing needs an element of continuity. Don't say one thing in the first paragraph, and then contradict it later. Numbers must add up, timelines need to be accurate and your data shared honestly. Think of threads running through a tapestry.
- *Convincing:* Present the case that you are an accomplished teacher. This means you present your evidence, and it is believable and achievable. The best way to do this is to include specific examples, documentation, rationales, and verification. Including specific examples provides stronger, more convincing evidence. *Examples = Evidence.*

What Works! Studying the Rubrics

- *Read* all of the levels from Level 4 down to Level 1. You will see a great difference in the quality of evidence described in each one.
- *Concentrate* on the Level 4 Rubric. Keep it beside you as you write so that you'll know exactly what evidence you need to show. Be sure you have evidence for each bullet. Notice how it aligns with parts of the Architecture of Accomplished Teaching. Also pay attention to presenting specific examples.
- *Use* the Level 4 Rubric to self-assess each component. Go through it bullet by bullet to be sure you've included everything you need. If something is missing, put it in!

Why It Works!

Using effective tools such as the *Architecture of Accomplished Teaching, SSTARS, and the Scoring Rubrics* will make the process less frustrating and more meaningful, because you'll know where to go for guidance and clarification. Make these tools work for you!

3 Getting Started and Getting Support

Six Word Memoir: Start sooner NOW, rather than later
LYNN, AZ

The Standards, The Lingo, and the Component Requirements:

New candidates often don't know where to start. They know they're embarking on a unique journey, but aren't sure what steps to take first. If this describes you, read on.

- Refresh your understanding of the Five Core Propositions. They are the umbrella under which all other National Board documents are organized.
- Read and internalize the NB Standards for your certificate. You must know what they look like in practice and how you use them in your practice.
- Read your *General Portfolio Instructions*. This is an underutilized resource with a wealth of information that is easy to refer to later.
- Study the *Learning Portfolio-Related Terms* (GLOSSARY) section in the General Portfolio Instructions to become familiar with National Board "language" that is specialized and specific to the National Board process. Certain phrases are used repeatedly in your instructions, and the glossary is where they are defined.
- Familiarize yourself with the Component Overviews at the beginning of your Portfolio Instructions to understand the content of each component.
- Study the *What Do I Need to Do?* section of each component for a list of component requirements.

What Works!

Familiarize yourself with the Portfolio Instructions, National Board "language," and structure of the component to give yourself the "big picture" and the tools and confidence to move forward.

Navigating the National Board Website:

The National Board website located at www.nbpts.org contains a wealth of information. Everything you want and need to know to complete Components 3 and 4 is there. But it is a complex site and not always easy to navigate. For the purposes of this chapter, I assume that everyone reading this is already a candidate, so I'll highlight the areas a candidate needs most. Here is a guide to its major components and the documents you'll need to find, download, print and refer to.

- From the homepage, click on the **For Candidates tab > First Time Candidates.** Now you are on a page with a matrix containing all the National Board documents. Click on the matrix to find:
- All the certificate areas.
- Component instructions which include the Scoring Rubrics and other Forms you'll submit.
- Certificate area National Board Standards
- Documents may be added or revised periodically, so always use the most current resource.
- Recently added features such as ATLAS, a video library of accomplished lessons, and HOMEROOM with many resources such as timelines and much more.

What Works!

These documents become your resources for mapping out your way through the National Board Certification Process. Becoming familiar with them will save time and grief!

Why These Works! Knowing where to go quickly for information is one way to work smart!

Organizing Your National Board Materials:

Once you have a basic overview of the components, it's time to implement some organizational strategies to help keep the myriad of written commentary drafts, paper piles, and artifacts you'll assemble. Here are several systems candidates have used successfully. Pick one or a combination that suits your own style and work habits.

What Works! Organizing KISS Options: (Keep It Super Simple!):

- Spiral-bind each set of component instructions. You'll end up with four "books" that are easy to carry reference. They are also sturdy and will stand up to heavy use. Your school may have a machine that does this operation or go to an office supply store.
- Keep instructions in a binder sectioned for each component. On the plus side, this keeps all instructions in one place. However, binders can be heavy and awkward to carry and pages can tear away from the rings. Still, it's a familiar organizational system for many candidates.
- Use a file box with sections or hanging folders for each component and for student work.

Why It Works!

Following a *KISS* system will be a lifesaver. You won't stress over the time you wasted hunting for lost work. Designate a place for your work—and keep it there!

What Works! Organizing Your Written Commentary on Your Computer

- Your computer is your best friend.
- Use a reliable word processing program: Word or Google Docs.
- Follow all instructions regarding font, type size, line spacing, margins, headers, and footers.
- Label each draft with the date. This will assure you are working on the latest version.

- Create a folder for each component and save drafts in their appropriate places.
- Periodically print out drafts or back them up on a flash drive/memory stick you can use on any computer. This step will save you a lot of stress if your computer crashes or your laptop is lost or stolen. You can also send your work to another computer.
- Remember: save early, save often, and save everything! Back up your files frequently.

Why It Works!

Doing everything you can to keep your writing accessible and safe is prudent and smart. Nothing is worse than losing what you've worked so hard to produce!

What Works! Organize Your Time

Figuring out how to organize your time is by far the most difficult challenge. As you well know, teachers are incredibly busy both at work and at home. Family and work continually compete for your time and energy. Here are some strategies successful candidates have used to help them cope with the time demands that National Board Certification places on them:

- *Just for this school year,* say no! Minimize as many committees and school responsibilities as possible. Promise your principal that you'll be back next year.
- *Just for this school year,* say no at home too. Delegate chores and activities. This is not the year to become Team Parent for all of your kids' sports teams and activities. Resign if you already are . . . spread the joy and let some other mom or dad take a turn.
- Set aside a designated daily or weekly work/writing period. Some candidates arrange for their spouse to be in charge of the family on a Saturday or Sunday afternoon, or for one weeknight. Other candidates stay late at school once a week or go to their classroom to work on the weekend. This is especially important from January to the deadline date.

- Consider arranging a weekend away from home so you can work undisturbed. Go to a hotel, a cabin, or house-sit for a friend who is away—anywhere you can be alone; OR send your family away!
- In the weeks before the deadline, you'll need additional time to finish and polish components. Plan for it.
- Create a flexible and realistic timeline and do your best to stick to it.

More Strategies

- Avoid procrastination; it will come back to haunt you. Some candidates say they work better under pressure, and that may be true *for a few*, but in the National Board process you can't quickly dash off a paper and produce a quality portfolio. The portfolio requires a great quantity of quality evidence collected over time, and putting together a successful portfolio is too complex to be done in a hurry.
- Be aware that you will need to work on more than one component at a time if you are tackling more than one component in a year.
- Look at your academic scope and sequence and begin to map out units for your components.
- Look at Component 3 and earmark lessons you teach that will fulfill the requirements.
- Save assessment data to use for Component 4.

Why It Works!

Organizing your time wisely can be a make-or-break factor in the quality of your portfolio submission.

Build a Support System: Cohort Support

When National Board Certification began, candidates were few and far between—both in numbers and location. It wasn't unusual for someone to be the only candidate in their entire state. Fortunately, few candidates face that kind of isolation today. Thanks to National Board Certified Teachers who have certified in the past, a continuum of support has developed across the country. Candidate support systems may be available in or near your school district.

If you are in a cohort, you will work with a Professional Learning Facilitator (PLF) or mentor who will guide your group and be obligated to provide and uphold ethical candidate support according to NBPTS guidelines.

Professional Learning Facilitator's Responsibilities:

- Help candidates understand the instructions and process more clearly.
- Help candidates think more clearly and deeply about their teaching practice.
- Help candidates learn to analyze the evidence presented.
- Help candidates engage in self-evaluation.
- Offer patience and encouragement.
- Guide candidates toward making their own decisions about evidence.
- Meet regularly with the candidate cohort and encourage peer collaboration.
- Share knowledge, skills, and experiences.
- Listen nonjudgmentally.
- Ask probing questions.
- Maintain confidentiality.

PLFs cannot:

- Guarantee a certifying score.
- Tell candidates their writing is wrong, flawed, not good enough, or that a component will or will not score well.
- Make a judgment call about portfolio instructions that seem unclear.
- Share NBCT portfolios or videos as teaching examples or tools.
- "Make" candidates into accomplished teachers or National Board Certified Teacher.
- Create evidence for candidates or tell them how to write the Written Commentary.

- Tell candidates which students to feature, which student work to submit, which videos to submit, or which segment of a video "will work" for sure.
- How to revise, edit, or fix a component.

If you participate in a cohort, you have responsibilities too... both to yourself and to the group.

Candidates' Responsibilities:

- Make an investment in time and attend scheduled meetings.
- Share fears, concerns, and issues.
- Continually read, review, and apply the standards.
- Bring work and questions to sessions.
- Keep to established timelines.
- Accept feedback in a professional manner.
- Study the component instructions.
- Come to meetings prepared.
- Maintain confidentiality.
- Commit time to the process.
- Celebrate steps along the way.

What Works!

If you don't have a cohort, you can still find support. Try these ideas:

- Form your own cohort. If there are other candidates in your district or area, organize a monthly meeting. Consider rotating the location so that all candidates host the group.
- Meet with other candidates outside your regular cohort meeting dates.
- Find online support. There are many National Board Facebook pages that offer reliable support:
    - National Board Certified Teacher - all certificate areas
    - National Board Certified Teachers on Facebook—all certificate areas

- NBCT Support—all certificate areas
- National Board Certification Survival Group—all certificate areas
- National Board Certification for English Teachers
- MCGen National Board Support
- Exceptional Needs—NBCTs and Candidates
- National Board Certification for World Language Teachers
- NBCT Social Studies Support Group
- NBCT EA/AYA Science
- National Board Certification—CTE
- National Board Certification—EMC Literacy
- English as a New Language NBCT—Candidates

These pages were all active at the time of the writing of this book. There may be other certificate-specific pages. Do a search. Some certificate-specific pages may not be as active as the pages for all certification.

Why It Works!

Collaborating with others gives you a sounding board and a place to ask questions and hear others' perspectives. Getting organized with a system that is user-friendly may take some trial and error. Once you find one that works for you, you'll feel more secure about moving forward.

4 Writing for the National Board

Six Word Memoir: Abandon beautiful wordage for Clear, Consistent, Convincing
KRISTIN, AR

Present Your Case

Writing National Board entries is unlike any other kind of writing you've done. It's not like the creative writing assignments you did in high school or college. It's not even like writing a term paper or master's thesis. Your score isn't determined by your grammar or sentence structure, fancy language or the number of research citations you include. In fact, some attributes of what is typically considered "good writing" don't necessarily apply here. So, what is it like?

Writing for the National Board is, above all else, *evidentiary*, meaning written to present *evidence*. Your sole purpose is to present evidence of your accomplished teaching, learning, leadership, and collaboration. It isn't quite as easy as pie, but it isn't rocket science either. You must make a case for your accomplished teaching the same way a lawyer argues a case in the courtroom—by presenting strong *evidence*. You are the defendant acting as your own attorney, presenting evidence of what you do in your classroom. Your student work samples, videos, and responses to the prompts are the evidence of your accomplished teaching. The assessor is the judge and jury.

Overview of the Three Styles of Writing: Description, Analysis, and Reflection

Just as an attorney uses questioning styles to elicit evidence, the National Board uses writing styles that can be explained in three verbs: *describe*, *analyze*, and *reflect*. Each prompt connects to one or more writing styles to help you present information that is *clear, consistent,* and *convincing. Describe, analyze,* and *reflect* are verbs that tell what you must *do*. The noun forms, *description, analysis,* and *reflection,* are the *results* of your actions.

Description Tells What

When you describe something, you tell *about* it; you tell *what* occurred. In court, a witness gives the facts in order to paint a clear picture of a situation. There should be no interpretation or judgment in descriptive writing. In a National Board entry, you respond with enough information for the assessor to form a picture or impression of what you want to depict. Key words in prompts that ask for description include:

- Tell
- Explain
- List
- Describe
- What … ?

A descriptive passage:

- Tells or retells the main facts.
- Is logically ordered.
- Has enough detail to set the scene and give assessors a basic sense of the class, student, or situation you need to describe.
- Contains accurate, precise enumeration wherever appropriate.
- Includes elements and features that allow an assessor to "see what you see."
- May be used in conjunction with analysis. You often need to describe the subject or situation you are analyzing so that it is visible to the assessor, making the analysis more meaningful. However, the borders between them can be fuzzy.

Description in the Writing:

Description is the easiest type of writing to do. Most teachers find description easy to write and typically tend to describe way too much. Although it is important to use description to give the facts and paint a picture of your class, students and activities, it isn't the most important type of writing. Why? *It is the least evidentiary of the writing styles.* Description sets the tone, draws a picture, and gives the facts. But it doesn't deliver much, if any, evidence. That is the task of analysis and reflection. Keep description at a minimum.

The **Instructional Context** section of Component 2, and any of the *Context Forms*, are the largest descriptive passages you will write. These give assessors a sense of your teaching context and the featured class and student(s). Tell enough to give the assessors a realistic picture of the characteristics that shape your teaching and the personality of the class. Be sure to respond to *every part* of each prompt, but keep as close to page suggestion as possible (one page in most certificates, two pages in some) because you'll need space later for other, more evidence-rich sections of the entries. Here are some *hypothetical* descriptive passages that might be found in an Instructional Context:

- *EA/Science:* The featured class consists of twenty-seven students, who are eleven to fourteen years old. Science is the first period of the day and several students are habitually tardy, which makes it difficult to begin instruction on time. Seven students are English Language Learners who leave ten minutes early to go to the Resource Room for language instruction. Therefore I must complete the essential lesson elements before they go.
- *MC/Generalist:* Jenny is both young and immature for a fourth grader. She reads at a second grade level and has particular trouble putting her thoughts on paper. She often misspells words and writes entire stories without using any punctuation. She likes to work with a partner but has difficulty staying focused on the task.
- *AYA/Math:* All students in this AP Statistics class plan to attend a four-year college. All students in the class have passed Algebra 2, and some are currently enrolled in Calculus 3. Nearly half of the students have taken an AP course before, but none have taken any statistics courses prior to this class.
- *EA/YA/Career and Technical Education:* The learners in this computer class vary in their linguistic and academic abilities, and state reading scores. The majority of students are in the "Basic" reading category which is below grade level. Four students are "Below Basic" which signifies they are far below grade level. Only one student in the whole

class is "Proficient" and on grade level. The class personality is pleasant and co-operative, and most students are generally on-task.

Keep these points in mind when describing.

- Be succinct. Say enough to paint the picture then stop.
- Decide which facts and details are significant and emphasize those.
- Concentrate on facts and details that show an impact on teaching or learning.
- Resist the urge to tell *everything*. Details matter, but don't go on and on.
- Description should be the smallest portion of your writing.
- Follow suggested page limits. They are there for a reason—to keep you from writing too much description and not enough analysis and reflection.
- Support the description with details and examples but not too many.

Analysis Asks So What and Why?

Description is the writing style that tells *what*. Analysis is the writing style that asks *so what?* and *why?* Compare it to an attorney who puts forth a theory, then goes about confirming or rejecting it depending on the evidence. Teachers make hundreds of decisions each day that are implicit in their knowledge of their students and content area, but seldom need to express this minutia orally or in writing. However, the analysis questions in each entry require this intrinsic knowledge be put into words on paper. Analytical writing is important because:

- It is the most evidentiary of the three styles.
- It demonstrates significance: *so what?* and *why?*
- It shows the assessor the reasons and motives (rationale) for your actions and decisions.
- It interprets and justifies actions and decisions backed up with evidence.

- It shows the assessor the thought processes you used to reach decisions.
- It examines why elements or events are described in certain ways.
- It involves taking apart what occurred during a teaching event.

Prompts that ask for analysis may contain these key words:

- How?
- Why?
- In what ways . . . ?
- Tell your rationale for . . .
- Explain why . . .

What Works! Use These Sentence Starters for Analytical Responses:

- Because I know ___, I __ (planned, provided, organized, taught . . .), which shows. . .
- I chose ___ because . . .
- There are several reasons why . . .
- The ___ on his paper showed me that he didn't understand ___, so I . . .
- The rationale behind my decision to ___ was . . .
- This was significant because . . .
- This impacted student learning by . . .
- Because ___, therefore . . .
- In order to ___, I . . .

The subject(s) being analyzed (student work samples or a video) must be available and visible to the assessors. Clearly label your student work samples and/or video and refer to them in the text. Assessors will look at the student work samples and videos to compare them to the evidence in your analysis. Typically, the assessor reads your entry, looks at the work samples or video to see how they support your writing and "match up," and then may read the entry again. The analysis helps the assessors see the significance of the evidence you submit.

Reflection Asks Now What?

The descriptive style of writing tells *what*, like a witness giving testimony or a journalist. The analytical style asks *so what* and *why*, like an attorney questioning a witness or a scientist. The reflective style goes a step further and asks *now what*? Reflection is like a jury looking back at the evidence to decide a case or a follow-up visit to a doctor to monitor a course of treatment. Reflection is a kind of self-analysis that:

- Explains the thought processes used *after* teaching a lesson/unit.
- Tells how you would make decisions in the future.
- Is retrospective.
- Explains the significance of a decision.
- Tells the impact of a decision, activity, or action.
- Reviews instructional strategy choices.
- Sets new goals based on your analytical conclusions.
- Demonstrates your understanding of the National Board Standards.

Prompts that require reflection ask you to look back at your teaching practice and/or to look ahead and predict what you might do differently. Analysis and reflection often overlap. Reflective prompts may ask you to make a judgment about:

- What would you do differently if you were to teach the lesson again?
- What does the featured student's performance suggest about your teaching practice?
- Were these goals appropriate? Why?
- Were your lesson design, strategies, and materials appropriate? How do you know?
- How did students perform in light of the chosen goals?
- Could I have taken this a step further to increase student understanding?
- What did I learn from this experience that will help me do even better next time?
- What did I learn about my teaching practice in relation to student learning?

Reflection assumes that analysis has already taken place. A typical mistake teachers make is to *retell*, rather than *reflect*. When you reflect, you *explain* and *interpret* what happened, *then* tell what should come next. You look back then forward.

Use These Pointers for Reflection:

- *Be honest*. There is always something that can be done better. No lesson is perfect.
- *Be realistic*. Don't propose something that is clearly impossible.
- *Focus* on both strengths and weaknesses of a lesson. No lesson is a total failure.
- *Use* concrete evidence to support your statements.
- *Align* and connect your instructional goals, the assessment activity, and your reflection on the lesson. There must be total consistency and agreement among them.
- *Focus* on the impact your teaching had on your students.

What Works! Using These Sentence Starters for Reflective Responses:

- In the future I . . .
- A key success was . . .
- An area for improvement is . . .
- My plan for the next lesson is . . .
- If I were to do this again . . .
- I learned ___ which will help me plan better next time by . . .
- Before this lesson my students. . ., but because of this experience . . .
- Because of this teaching experience, I learned. . .

Why These Work! The boundaries between analysis and reflection are not always clear-cut. Analysis focuses on *so what?*, reflection focuses on *now what?* Analysis is about the past; reflection is about using the past to determine future actions. Understanding reflection will make your writing stronger.

Evidence or Lack of Evidence in Your Writing:

Read and reflect on the following samples to see if you can tell the difference in the amount of evidence presented in each pair of examples:

- **#1-Lack of Evidence**: Rory had trouble writing complete responses to comprehension questions, so I gave him a graphic organizer to help him organize his thoughts and information.
- **#1-With Evidence**: I planned a reading comprehension activity. I directed students to read a text and answer questions. Rory was unable to write responses in complete sentences, and he also skipped questions. To determine Rory's reading level, I administered the DRA (Developmental Reading Assessment). I learned he could answer questions orally but struggled to put his thoughts on paper. Rory shared that when he saw a list of questions he felt overwhelmed, so I began having him use a graphic organizer I designed that allowed him to record information in shortened form . . .
- **#2-Lack of Evidence**: My classroom is set up so kids can get their own supplies. One student from each group got supplies for their group. Each group set up their ramp and started rolling their cars down it to see how far they would travel. Marci's group rolled a car down their ramp, and it traveled a yard. They knew this, because they measured with their string and a yardstick.
- **#2-With Evidence**: I set up my science lab and centers for easy access to materials and to give adequate space for the inquiry activity. Marci was easily able to retrieve the materials her group needed to measure the distance their car rolled off their ramp. She and her group also had space to place their ramp and have room for the car to roll. When the car came to a stop, they used the string to measure from the bottom of the ramp to the front end of the car. Then they laid the string on a yardstick to measure the distance in inches and feet. Sam measured and declared the distance to be 3 feet. Lynn said, "That is a yard. Our car traveled a yard!" I asked others in the group if they agreed. Marci replied, "Yes, 3 feet is the same as a yard." This showed me everyone in that group understood the measuring equivalents.
- **#3-Lack of Evidence**: I used materials and realia from Mexico, Costa Rica, Spain, and Panama for this lesson to provide a more concrete visual of the foreign country.

- **#3-With Evidence**: I used a variety of authentic materials and realia for this lesson to provide a more concrete visual of the foreign country. My bulletin board was covered with a map of Mexico, pictures from a Costa Rican calendar, newspapers from Spain, posters from a travel company, photographs from books, and magazine ads promoting Panama as a tour destination.

What Works!

Give specific examples in your written commentary to give a clear, consistent, and convincing picture of your accomplished teaching. *EXAMPLES = EVIDENCE.*

Why This Works! Examples build a strong wall of evidence!

Danger! Style Faux Pas and Pitfalls:

While learning to write with the three styles, some writing hazards emerge. Watch out for these and avoid them:

- **Missing Person Alert** Q: What is missing from this hypothetical passage?

    The students were introduced to their new vocabulary by using flashcards. After practicing as a whole group, they were divided into study groups. First they were assigned jobs within the group. Each group was provided with a set of flashcards and a worksheet to reinforce their learning. After all of the groups finished, we discussed the words again. Then each was assigned words to use in a sentence and illustrate.

    Q: *What is wrong with the above passage?* A: **The teacher is missing**! Nowhere in that passage is the teacher mentioned. Who is the teacher? Where is the teacher? When writing your entries, don't hide in the background, be invisible. You must put yourself in the picture—clearly, consistently, and convincingly. How do you do that?

    How to fix it: *Write in the first person!* **I** introduced students to their new vocabulary using flash cards. After practicing as a whole group, **I** divided them into study groups. First **I** assigned jobs within the group then **I** provided a set of flashcards and worksheet to reinforce their learning. After all of the groups finished, **I** led a discussion about the words and assigned words to use in a sentence and illustrate.

What Works! Making Yourself Visible Within Your Writing:

- Write in the first person. Use the pronoun *I* frequently. Candidates often feel that writing about themselves is bragging, and that feels uncomfortable. Put those feeling aside and use first person pronouns in order to showcase your actions.
- Be careful with the pronoun **we**. It takes more space, but it is stronger to say, the students and I, rather than **we**. That way it's clear just who **we** are; *you* are in the picture.
- Use **we** sparingly. Use it once, then switch back to *I*.
- In Component 4, when using **we** to show collaboration, use it once, then turn the focus to your own contribution and switch to *I* or **my**: *I* collaborated with my department to plan the science fair. **We** each had assigned roles. **My** role was to...
- Use the active voice because it is clearer, more direct, and more concise. Go back and look at the example passage. Not only is the teacher missing, the verbs are almost all written in the passive voice. Sentences using passive voice verbs are wordier, longer, and less clear than those using the active voice. The *fixed* example uses active voice verbs.
- Use **helping verbs, by** and **–ing** endings sparingly. For example say: *I provided flashcards*... instead of *Flashcards were provided*... or *I was providing*... After writing a draft, go back and highlight each verb phrase with a helper and/or –ing. Then rewrite as many as possible in the active voice.

Look again at the rewritten passage with pronouns that put the teacher into the picture and with active voice verbs. Do you see the differences?

Why This Works!

This passage is much stronger because the teacher is clearly in the picture, and the active voice verbs show who performed the actions expressed. There are also details to demonstrate how this teacher's actions support the National Board Standards. This lets the assessor know who led the lesson and how the teacher produced learning.

More Writing Faux Pas and Pitfalls:

- **Preaching from the Pulpit**: This occurs when the candidate uses the written commentary as a soapbox. Avoid inserting personal views and frustrations about teaching into the written commentary. It is a waste of words and space. In a nutshell, accomplished teachers are able to demonstrate accomplished teaching and student learning in spite of difficulties and obstacles. Assessors score only *evidence* of accomplished teaching, so it is important to use words and space to demonstrate your evidence.

- **The E.S.P. Communicator**: When candidates don't explain their actions and decisions clearly, the assessor is left to connect the dots. Be careful not to assume that the reasons for choices are so obvious that no explanation is needed. Some candidates may be clear about what they **do**, but they may write ambiguously or not at all about the thinking processes that led them to a particular decision. This is a common pitfall, especially among more experienced candidates whose actions have become so intuitive and automatic that they no longer deliberately think about the reasons for their decisions.

    It may seem tedious or annoying to be pressed into the deeper thinking that the analysis and reflection sections require. But you must explain the thinking and decision making processes you applied to student work samples, videos or other artifacts used in the entries. Never assume that an assessor will **see** evidence without an explanation. Explain your decisions and choices.

- **The Feelings Guru**: This candidate substitutes feelings for concrete evidence. Work to eliminate all *I believe, I feel, I tried, and I think* statements from your writing. Although teachers are very caring people, the National Board entries are not the place to lay out your personal teaching philosophy or beliefs. Statements such as *I believe all children can learn . . .* or *I feel that all students should . . .* , however true, are irrelevant to the process. The assessor looks for **evidence** of a teacher's effectiveness, but a teacher's philosophy is not a measurable piece of evidence. Assessors look for evidence in the form of specific examples, descriptions, analysis, reflection, and artifacts such as student work samples and videos. Avoid these pitfalls by returning to the trial lawyer analogy. You must present evidence clearly, convincingly, and consistently to the assessors who are the judge and jury.

- ***Jargon***: It is the specialized language, words, and terms used within a profession. Use it sparingly. Too much educational jargon gets in the way of understanding. The best writing is plain, simple easily understood language—the kind you use when you talk.

What Works! Using Strong Verbs, Strong Phrases, and Bloom's Taxonomy

Writing strong National Board entries does not require a fancy vocabulary. The assessors come from all fifty states, big cities and small towns and are teachers just like you. Ask yourself whether anyone, from anywhere, will understand what you wrote and you'll be on the right track.

Strong verbs and Phrases describe accomplished teaching actions and qualities that have meaning within the National Board Certification process. They are words that help you showcase your teaching practice as described in the Standards. They are, for the most part, plain, strong verbs and descriptive phrases. Using these verbs and phrases in your writing can lend clarity and strength to your descriptions, analyses and reflections. But the criteria for using them are authenticity and honesty. They must have meaning within the context of your teaching practice. Here are some examples:

- **Strong Verbs**: I encouraged, developed, designed, guided, supported, organized, facilitated, chose, chose to, selected, challenged, provided, gave, taught, engaged, demonstrated, learned, modeled, measured, asked, practiced, assigned, performed, contributed, impacted, influenced, instructed, questioned
- **Strong Phrases**: students as risk-takers; ways of learning; learning community; lifelong learner; build self-esteem; promote student understanding; appropriate assessment; constructive feedback; fairness; equity; goal related; integrated learning; behavior intervention; active engagement/listening; high expectations; insightful questions; meaningful; learning goals; outcome based; reluctant learner; on task; rich and in-depth; inclusion; productive classroom; cooperative groups; parent partnerships.
- **More Strong Phrases**: community involvement; collaboration; diverse perspectives;

beyond the classroom; high expectations; problem solving; real-world applications; rich variety of sources; student ownership; teacher as a learner; teaching strategies; unique learning needs; varied assessments; work collaboratively; standards based; content oriented; application; direct impact on student learning; I learned; I should have; now I understand; relevant characteristics; and motivational.

- *Bloom's Taxonomy* is one of the best references for finding effective verbs that indicate levels of learning and for planning appropriate lessons. Here is a recap (lowest to highest levels):
- *Remembering*: define, memorize, record, identify, label, list, locate, match, name, recall, spell, tell, state, underline, recognize, repeat
- *Understanding:* restate, discuss, describe, explain, express, identify, interpret, paraphrase, put in order, restate, retell, summarize, review
- *Applying:* apply, conclude, construct, use, dramatize, illustrate, show, sketch, draw, give a new example, solve, operate, practice, translate
- *Analyzing:* distinguish, analyze, differentiate, appraise, experiment, compare, contrast, diagram, debate, categorize, classify, dissect, infer
- *Evaluating:* defend, judge, value, evaluate, support, argue, appraise
- *Creating:* assemble, construct, create, design, develop, formulate, write

Why These Work!

These verbs provide evidence in your writing. They indicate your deliberate participation in the processes that make up accomplished teaching and are examples of the "language" used in the Standards that show evidence of accomplished teaching. Apply the litmus test to decide if something meets the criteria for being universally understood. There must be no confusion about the terms used in the written commentary. This is especially true for the names of programs or materials you or your school utilizes. Be sure to spell them out and give a brief explanation.

Examples:

- Career Ladder, a pay-for-performance program . . .
- NCTM, the National Council of Teachers of Mathematics

What Works! Creating a Writing Framework

- Make the case that you are an accomplished teacher by showing evidence of exemplary teaching. You are the lawyer. The assessors are the judge and jury.
- Connect the three styles of writing to the prompts: description, analysis, and reflection.
- Keep description to a minimum. Description tells *what*.
- Analysis asks *so what?* and *why?* and is the most evidentiary type of writing.
- Reflection asks *now what?* and is a type of self-analysis.
- Provide concrete examples of your actions and decisions.
- Write in the first person as much as possible.
- Use strong verbs and the active voice.
- Avoid using large amounts of educational jargon.
- Use buzz verbs, buzz phrases, and Bloom's Taxonomy language wherever appropriate.
- Be authentic.

Why These Work!

Your writing is the "legal brief" of your portfolio. It contains all the evidence to show the assessors that you are an accomplished teacher.

What Works! Following the 3Cs in the Level 4 Rubric:

- *Clear:* Never assume anything and explain everything.
- *Consistent:* Goals, activities, assessments, and so on must match up and be connected.
- *Convincing*: Build a wall of evidence with examples.

Add more Cs:

- *Concise:* Make your point and move on. Write short, to-the-point sentences.

- *Correct:* Use correct grammar and punctuation so that the assessor can focus on your content.
- *Concrete:* Evidence needs to be specific, real, and measurable, not vague and ambiguous.

Style Tips:

- Limit bolding, underlining, and CAPS. A little goes a long way.
- Be as consistent as possible with verb tenses.
- Talk to the assessor, not at the assessor. The assessor is your audience.
- Write in your own voice. Don't lose yourself in the writing process.
- State the *significance* of events.
- Avoid acronyms unless you are sure the assessor will understand them or can explain them.
- Streamline writing and cut the fluff. Edit! Edit! Edit numerous times!
- Avoid *helping verbs* and *–ing* forms of verbs wherever possible.

Be Sure To:

- Back up your writing on your computer often!
- Pay attention to page limits. Assessors can read only the required number of pages.
- Answer *all* parts of every question/prompt. Respond *to* the question, not *about* it.
- Show impact on student learning.
- Connect your teaching practice to the Standards.
- Study the Architecture of Accomplished Teaching for insight into the prompts.
- Give up stressing about the vagueness of the prompts. It will only drive you crazy.

Why These Work!

Clear, consistent, convincing writing showcases your evidence.

5 Component 3: Teaching Practice and Learning Environment
The Video Component

You know you are a National Board candidate when: You have made so many videos that you shop them to networks for an educational reality show.

Annie

You know you are a National Board candidate when: You get so comfortable filming that you confuse your classroom with the set of a reality show and make side comments to the camera.

Overview

Component 3, worth 30 percent of your score, uses two videos in all certificate areas to capture a snapshot of your instructional planning, your pedagogical knowledge and skills, and how successfully you apply these within your practice to advance student learning. It's the only component that lets the assessors truly see you in action. Components are scored holistically. This means the videos aren't scored separately from the writing but rather serve as *support* for your writing. They back up what you write with viewable evidence. For example, if you write that you fostered critical thinking by asking higher-level questions, and the assessors hear those kinds of questions in the video, you're creating *consistency* and your writing becomes more *convincing*. Assessors are trained to find evidence wherever it is . . . in the writing, on the forms, and in the videos. In a nutshell you:

- *Film* two videos, each highlighting different instructional formats.
- *Respond* to a set of prompts *for each video* in a written commentary.
- *Complete* three Forms.

Stressed Out:

Let's be honest. For most candidates, the video component creates a lot of stress. Most certificates require a total of two videos; however, some, such as Music, requires three. Note that the Music Component 2 requires a short video. Log onto any National Board Facebook page, group, or attend almost any cohort meeting and you'll find candidates struggling to get videos that "will work." When any group of candidates or NBCTs gather, horror stories about filming abound. Getting a workable video segment is paramount because the bulk of Component 3 can't be written until the videos are made and the segments are chosen.

Why Video?

Why does the National Board ask you to make videos?

- Videos offer particularly strong evidence of a candidate's pedagogical knowledge and ability to manage learning opportunities, because the videos are snapshots of real lessons in real time.
- Videos allow the candidate to be in charge of what an assessor sees—unlike a random drop-in surprise evaluation from an administrator. The assessor sees only what you choose to submit. Did a student get sick? Don't choose that part. Surprise fire drill while you are taping? Edit it out. You have the power and flexibility to determine what an assessor sees. Submitting videos is a gift, really, an opportunity to show your real teaching practice on your terms.
- Videos are the best way to showcase the climate of a classroom, teaching and management strategies, student engagement, the discourse environment, and the interactions that take place during teaching and learning sequences.
- Videos give assessors a real glimpse of your classroom as well as the opportunity to view a snapshot of your teaching and your students' learning. It's very difficult to film a lesson and sustain an environment that isn't real. A dog and pony show will become obvious to assessors very quickly.

Video Early

Starting early to video is a good thing. Film a few lessons just for practice. This takes the pressure off, gives you an opportunity to learn to use the equipment effectively, and gives your students and you the chance to get used to being filmed. It can be a good way to figure out some of the important logistics such as camera placement, sound issues, etc. It can also be a good idea for you and the class to watch some of the videos together. It helps give the kids a sense of filming etiquette and ownership and they can get some of their silliness or shyness out of the way. You can also become more comfortable being filmed.

Film Multiple, Whole Lessons

Plan to film more than one *real, complete* lesson—lessons you feel will show the interactions etc. you want to capture. Use the prompts and other information in your instructions, especially the yellow bullet points in the *Selecting a Lesson for Each Video* section of your instructions, to plan lessons that give opportunities for those elements to take place. Film whole lessons so you'll have segments to choose from within each lesson. Use what you've learned from your practice videos about camera placement to get the best views of students' faces (and yours) and adequate sound quality. With filming small groups within a larger group setting, , film yourself working with more than one group because you can't know in advance which group will provide the richest conversations and where the most evidence to write about will occur.

Filming Frustrations

Even though the rationale for making videos is powerful, getting one you want to use can be among the most frustrating aspects of the certification process. Why is that?

- Most of us hate seeing ourselves on video. We don't like our hair, our clothes, our weight, or our voices. We may discover vocal or physical mannerisms we weren't aware of and that we don't like. So a major obstacle is to *get over ourselves*. It takes some effort, but you can learn to concentrate on the content of the lesson instead of yourself. Consider it a major milestone when you conquer this hurdle.

- Technology and logistical issues can be frustrating and intimidating. Being unfamiliar with the equipment, arranging for someone to come in and film, and microphones that don't pick up the sound all cause angst. Add in cords that come unplugged, handling student behavioral concerns and a dead battery, and you have the recipe for a possible meltdown. Fortunately, you can have up to two edits for technical difficulties. More on that later.

Choosing Different Instructional Formats: A Most Important Decision!

You will submit videos of two lessons from different instructional units. Together the videos should show different formats. Format refers to:

- Different group sizes
- Different teaching strategies and activities
- Different content

You want to show yourself managing these differences successfully. You want to vary the instruction, content, and the group size seen in each video. Essentially, what this means is that you don't want to teach the two video lessons in the same way to same-size groups. First, you want to show you can manage and teach different sizes/configurations of groups. Your instructions list several options:

- Large/Whole Group
- Small Group
- 1:1
- Other appropriate configuration

Focus on a different-size group for each video. Group size can be used to determine the strategies you want to use. Next, focus on choosing different teaching strategies, content, and activities for each video that promotes active learning for the group sizes shown. Think about how to structure the lesson. Ask yourself:

- What will you do?
- What content will you cover?
- What materials will you need?
- What activities will the students do?
- How will you plan for interactions during the lessons?
- How will you interact with students and they with you?
- How will students interact with each other?
- What group size and instructional strategies will best address the purpose of the learning you want the students to experience?

The response to each question above should be *different* for Video 1 and Video 2.

Most teachers, over time, develop some favorite and effective systems or models for delivering lessons we use frequently. For example, a hypothetical lesson model might include an introduction, direct instruction, pair-share, independent work, review, and closure. Another model might be, *I Do* (teacher models info/activity), *We Do* (teacher and class complete practice together); *You Do* (student works independently). Of course, there are many variations of these models, many other ways to present lessons.

The point I'm making is *you don't want to submit both videos that use the same lesson structure/model or copycat strategies*. If you use a game activity in Video 1, use a discussion in Video 2. If you use turn-and-talk in Video 1, use manipulatives in Video 2. If Video 1 is about fractions, make the content of Video 2 different. In other words, make the *strategies* used in each video different. This allows assessors to see you have a tool-box of strategies to use according to the needs of the lesson.

Labeling/Naming the Format of a Video:

Sometimes labeling/naming a video is easy. A video showing a teacher working with one student is a 1:1 video; working with a pair-just call it that; or a video showing one small group pulled from a larger class/group to work on a specific skill, for the entirety of the video, is obviously a small-group video. A typical whole-class video shows a teacher teaching the whole class, all of whom are working on the same objective/task. But some configurations aren't as clearly defined and fall into a kind of gray area. Here are some common examples:

- A reading teacher or interventionist works with her whole group of three students. The group is small, but they constitute this teacher's whole group. If those students are all working on the same objective/task, then it would be considered a whole group video because the whole group is doing the same thing.
- A whole class is seen in a video, in the background, and the teacher pulls a group for separate instruction. That's a small-group video. The teacher is working only with that group for all or most of the video.
- A whole class is working on an objective/task. The students sit in table groups, and table groups work together during independent practice. Each group is doing the same task. The teacher walks around the room checking on groups, helping here and there. This would likely be considered a whole group video because all students have the same task and the teacher is monitoring the whole class.
- A teacher sets up stations. Students are divided into groups and rotate through the stations. All students visit all stations. Although students move in groups, all students have the same task and are essentially doing the same things. This would be a whole group video.
- A teacher sets up stations. Each station is part of a "jigsaw" activity where each group creates something that is later used along with what the other groups produce, to make a complete product/presentation. Each part is different and contributes to the whole. The teacher may move among groups, but because each group has a different task, this could be described as a small-group lesson.
- SCIENCE TEACHERS: *Lab* is one of the configurations listed in the Science Component three instructions, so you can just call this video a *LAB*. *Lab* is not listed specifically in other components.

These are examples where the label is generally agreed upon, but they don't fit every scenario. Not all situations are easy to label. If you sincerely think a certain teaching scenario is a particular format/configuration, and you can make a case for calling it that, you should do so. Write like an attorney and make your case. Give your rationale for your choice.

What Works!

Regardless of the label you put on a video, the most important aspect is that the two videos are *different from each other* in group size and teaching strategies.

Why This Works!

Making videos that show a variety of evidence, different group sizes and teaching strategies shows your depth of knowledge of pedagogy and content.

What Will the Videos Look Like?

Each ten- to fifteen-minute video will show you teaching and working with your students in either a whole/large group, a small group or groups, or with individuals 1:1, or another appropriate configuration such as pairs. You can focus on just one of those formats in each video or there could be mixed formats on one video. For example, you could begin a lesson with a whole group, then transition into small groups and rotate around the room to work with several during the lesson. You might choose a segment to submit that focuses on just ONE of those configurations (the whole group OR the small groups), or both could show. For example, you could show twelve minutes of whole group instruction, then show three minutes of small-group work. However, each video needs to have a clear format . . . mostly/all whole group, mostly/all small group, or mostly/all individual instruction etc., because this is the format you'll write about. You won't submit two videos that are mainly/totally whole group for example.

Conversely, a small-group video can feature you working with just one group the whole time, and the same for 1:1 instruction. I've seen fifteen minutes with one student, I've seen eight minutes with Student A and seven minutes with Student B. You can make these choices.

Editing Your Videos:

In the original process, any editing was completely forbidden. Now, however, there are three, and only three, allowable editing circumstances:

- Moving a *class* into a different instructional setting, such as a lab, a gym, a library, or outdoors. Transitioning from whole group to small group, from the rug to table groups etc. does NOT fit this circumstance.
- Responding to a *safety drill*. This does NOT include someone knocking on the door, being interrupted with announcements, or someone entering or leaving your room.
- Changing the battery in the video camera. This does not apply to a camera or iPad that comes unplugged, microphones that aren't plugged in, or a phone without enough charge.

Although each video is allowed *up to* two, very specific edits for three purposes, the safest and best scenario is one with NO edits. Do all you can to make that your goal. For each edit, you must note the reason on the Instructional Planning Form. If a video with more than two edits is submitted, only the segment *before* the third edit will be viewed and considered in the scoring. If a video contains non-allowable edits, *the video will not be scored*. The ability to edit can be a gift, but use it judiciously.

What Works! Video Smart!

What most candidates struggle with is wanting to film a perfect lesson. However, the lesson you submit doesn't have to be perfect—seriously! Neither do your students nor yourself! In fact, a "perfect" video could give the appearance of being staged. The assessors aren't looking for a dog and pony show; they expect to see a real lesson. *Fake* almost always backfires in some way. *Genuine* gives honest data to write about. The best way to *video smart* is to understand the prompts, learn what the assessors expect to see and plan a lesson that gives opportunities for those aspects to show. That is how you demonstrate the NB Standards in your teaching practice.

What Works! Design the Lesson with the End in Mind: Plan Backwards

Like when planning the student work component, an effective way to get a video that works is to plan *backwards*. Know your destination, and then plan how to get there. Instead of blindly videotaping (except for the initial practice sessions) and hoping the evidence is there, begin with the prompts and the evidence you need to demonstrate—then plan how to include that evidence in your lesson.

Selecting the Video Lesson and Segment

In the *Selecting a Lesson for Each Video* section of all Component 3 certificate instructions, there are several subheadings and bullet points addressing the areas of Learning Environment, Student Engagement, and Instruction. Studying these and incorporating as many as possible into your planning and video can strengthen to your videos—and your writing. Many bullet points are similar or identical from one certificate to another, but some are subject-specific. Example:

- *All Certificates:* LEARNING ENVIRONMENT: Create a student-centered learning environment based on trust and mutual respect.
- *Art:* INSTRUCTION: Integrate art-making, studying, interpreting, and evaluation activities that are connected to learning goals, and sequence structure instruction so that students can achieve the goals.
- *EA/AYA English Language Arts:* INSTRUCTION: Support all students in developing the dispositions and proficiencies necessary for comprehending, analyzing, evaluating, and appreciating text; making a product communicate its intended meaning; and advancing the students' speaking and listening abilities so they engage in meaningful conversations with a variety of audiences and purposes.
- *MCGen:* STUDENT ENGAGEMENT: Foster the active engagement of students with the teacher and each other in sharing ideas, conversing purposefully, and listening attentively as they explore significant topics relevant to middle childhood curricula.

Create opportunities within the lesson(s) you plan for these elements to take place. They are all based on one or more NB Standards, so when these show in a video and you write about them, you are demonstrating concrete evidence of the NB Standards. Some evidence of these points will be:

- Words/conversations you and/or the students say
- Product produced
- Technology used.

Other evidence may be more subtle. For example, what evidence might be observed to know there is a safe, fair, equitable, and challenging environment that promotes active student engagement?

- Are students comfortable speaking and responding to questions and to each other?
- Do all students have the opportunity to participate?
- Is some differentiation evident?
- Is the topic appropriate for the students?

Those are more subtle signs you may need to dig deeper to find. Evaluating these aspects may send you back to your Standards to read again and highlight examples.

What Works! Filming the Lesson

The information contained in your NBPTS GENERAL instructions and within the component regarding filming techniques is comprehensive and the definitive word. But here is a list of additional tips.

- *Get* release forms signed and kept in a safe place for all students and adults being filmed. Back-to-school night is a great time to do this. Those without permission can be seated out of camera range. Keep forms until your certificate expires or you complete the MOC (Maintenance of Certificate) process 5 years after initial certification.
- *Learn* to ignore the camera and teach your students to do the same. Set the camera up often, so that it becomes just another object in the room.

- *Consider* having a student operate the camera when it is on a tripod.
- *Consider* setting the tripod at student eye level when filming small groups, which may mean placing the camera on a low table or even the floor.
- *Have* sturdy extension cords available and use them safely (taped to the floor).
- *Use* an external microphone with groups if possible.
- *Show* the faces of the students and the teacher.
- The teacher must appear clearly at least once within the segment submitted, but does not have to show every minute. Tell your videographer to film your face at least every 5 minutes. If filming yourself, move into camera range several times during the lesson.
- The camera should focus on students to showcase their discussion and actions.
- Don't make the video all "teacher talk."
- Don't "stage" any lesson. "Real" is honest, more natural, and gives you real material to write about. "Fake" is unethical and almost always backfires.
- Turn off fans, aquarium pumps, etc. when possible to avoid extraneous noise.
- Pay attention to what you wear. The assessors receive bias training, but you still want to appear professional. Think about what might be hanging out, hanging over, or showing when you bend over.
- Allow yourself one "pity party" to moan and groan about your hair, your voice, your weight, or whatever other faults you perceive you have. Then get over yourself so you can focus on the content of the video!
- *The biggest video mistakes*: The teacher talks too much, not enough student-to-student talk, too much procedural talk, not enough content talk, not enough student-to-student interaction.

More Filming Tips

- Read your directions very carefully so that you know exactly what grouping Component 3 suggests for your certificate area. The instructions are the final word!

- If you have no videographer, place the camera on a tripod near a *front corner* to film a whole group. You can pick up the tripod move the camera whenever needed.
- Carry the camera to a location, set the camera down to capture a group working, and walk in and out of the frame if needed. Turn the camera around occasionally to show yourself.
- The camera can be on a tripod focused on one location, students at a table for example, and groups can move to and from the table. You can show *short* transitions. Have the videographer follow you from group to group, but it's permissible for them to also pan the room occasionally or focus on one group for an interval.
- Do everything possible to have student voices heard. It helps the assessors and saves you from needing to do extensive transcription in the writing. Consider investing in a portable microphone.

The video is *support for your written commentary* and doesn't need to be perfect. Plan your logistics for filming, but keep them as simple as possible.

Unpacking the Prompts: What Do They Ask?

Determine what the outcome of each prompt might look like in a video. Two prompts directly ask you to cite evidence from the video, so it's important you refer to specific places in the video where the examples are seen/heard.

1) ***What specific approaches, strategies, techniques, or activities did you use to promote active student engagement in the lesson? Cite specific examples from the video recording.***

    - All certificate areas have these two prompts. *Approaches, strategies, techniques, and activities* are plural, so explain more than one. Notice the *or* in the prompt. If there is more than one activity, consider having them use different learning modalities so more than one way to learn is visible. Here are some strategies to consider:
        - Questioning
        - Paraphrasing
        - Cooperative Learning Groups

- Pair-Share
- Socratic Seminar
- Fishbowl
- Discussion
- Quick Writes
- Demonstration/Modeling
- Using a Manipulative
- Technology

2) **To what extent did you achieve the lesson's goal or goals? Provide evidence from the video recording to support your answer.** The opening phrase asks for a *quantity*—to what extent? Evidence for this could be shown in several ways:

- In an evaluation.
- What students **say**—to each other and/or to you. *When Juan could tell his partner something, I knew he had achieved the goal of the lesson.*
- What students **do**. *I saw that Sandra was able to ___, thus achieving the lesson's goals.*

Citing direct evidence from the video for these two prompts is **non-negotiable**. The assessors *must* be able to see these specific examples, and they must be documented in your writing. This supports the *consistency* element of the scoring rubric. Citing evidence for these prompts strengthens your responses and it's more *likely* you'll have a useable video.

Once you have a segment that you feel shows evidence for those two prompts, it may be worth the time to do some scripting. Thinking of what needs to show, make a list of:

- Strategies you see yourself using (questions, paraphrasing, modeling, etc.)
- Words kids say when conversations and/or responses take place.
- Actions students take during an activity and the results.

But wait! There's more! Here are some thinking points for the remaining prompts found in *most* certificate areas (some certificate areas may vary—so check yours!):

How did you establish a safe, fair, equitable, and challenging learning environment for all students? This prompt BEGS you to refer back to your NB Standard regarding fairness, equity, and diversity to understand what each means and how each might look in a classroom. Think about:

- *Safe* can refer to both physical and emotional safety; *equity* refers to being fair and impartial and giving/getting what is needed. What do you do in your classroom to ensure these are in place?
- What routines and/or expectations are in place that might contribute to these factors?
- How do you challenge bias and encourage your students to do the same?
- How does your instruction provide challenges while remaining sensitive to students' developmental levels?

How did you monitor and assess student progress during the lesson, and how did this influence your decision making during instruction? How was student feedback provided and what was your rationale for providing it in this manner? Think about:

- How do you monitor student progress, both during instruction and over a unit of study?
- How do you monitor groups and individuals?
- What formative strategies do you use day to day to assess?
- What summative instruments measure student learning and growth?
- What types of feedback do you give? Oral? Written? Peer?
- Is your feedback meaningful—beyond "good job"?
- Will your feedback help students move forward?
- How does your feedback help students assess their own progress?
- How does your feedback from one assignment help students do better on another assignment?
- Is your feedback targeted and specific, or general and vague?
- WHY do you provide feedback in this (these) way?

How was your approach to teaching this content to the students in this video influenced by past experience? Think about:

- If you've taught this content before, how did that experience contribute to decisions you made while planning this lesson?
- Did you make changes based on previous experiences? If so, what kinds?
- Do these students, at this time, in this place, exhibit characteristics that made modifications of past teaching necessary?

What would you do differently, if anything, if you are to teach this particular lesson again to a similar group of students next year? If you would not change anything, explain why. This may be one of the more important prompts because it's heavily reflective. Reflection requires you to look back and analyze, then use that knowledge to look ahead.

- Reflection means to think deeply and carefully about something.
- Reflection contributes to effectiveness.
- How can you apply this deep thinking to impact student learning in the future?
- Reflection needs to ultimately be student-centered. Modifying teaching strategies ultimately impacts student learning.
- Reflect on your knowledge of your students and content to gauge the effectiveness of your practice.
- How can you help your students reflect on their learning to strengthen your impact?

There is no such thing as a perfect lesson. The NB expects you to look for ways to make your lessons better. If you claim the lesson(s) on the video was perfect, you need to be able to fully explain why. For our purposes, we'll assume some improvement is possible, so if you did this lesson again, knowing what you know now, what could be changed that might impact student learning?

- Modify time frame?
- Reconfigure groups?
- Use different resources?
- Modify content?
- Address more/different learning styles?
- Differentiate instruction?

- Monitor/assess differently?
- Less teacher talk?
- More direct instruction?
- Should we investigate students' prior exposure to content before planning?

What Assessors Expect to See: Use the Prompts and Rubric Statements:

This is what every candidate wants to know-what are the assessors looking for? It's not a secret; the clues are in the instructions, prompts, and rubric statements, and ask for evidence such as:

- The goal/objective matches the instructions seen on the video.
- Multiple teaching strategies, methods, or activities are evidenced.
- Teacher to student interaction occurs.
- Student to teacher interaction occurs.
- Student-to-student interaction occurs.
- Fairness, equity, access, and respect for diversity are evident.

What Works! Finding the Evidence Assessors Expect to See: Sample Lessons.

- *The goal matches the activity.* Goal: Students learn about Newton's Laws of Motion (science). Activity: Students roll small cars down ramps covered with various surfaces to gather data about how the surface of a ramp can affect the cars; speed and distance.

Compare that example to a real example with a disconnect between the goal and the activities:

A kindergarten teacher plans a unit on the life cycle of pumpkins (it's autumn!). She sets up a variety of centers for her students to explore. At the centers students count pumpkin seeds, use puppets to act out a rhyme about *"5 Little Pumpkins,"* listen to a recorded story, and sample pumpkin foods. They LOVE these activities ... but when this scenario was submitted, it didn't score well. WHY? Not one of those centers had any connections to a pumpkin's *life cycle*! The goal and the activities didn't match.

- *Multiple strategies/options are evident.* Some students prepare ramps with various surfaces for an inquiry activity, while others are engaged in snapping together Unifix cubes to use for measurement and gather cars to roll down the ramps. Everyone writes their observations in their science journal. There is choice and/or differentiation of tasks and information is presented in more than one way: perhaps in the forms of reading text, discussion, and a video. To provide differentiation, students have the choice of measuring in varying ways—with the Unifix cubes or a ruler/meter/yard stick for example.
- *Teacher to student interaction*: The teacher engages students in discourse about the motion of the cars as they roll down the ramp, asks open-ended questions, and asks them to compare, evaluate, explain or defend an answer/approach.
- *Student to teacher interaction*: A student question or comment may spark a back-and-forth exchange. The teacher has comments or questions ready to encourage responses and notes misconceptions or interactions that occur that indicate understanding.
- *Student-to-student interaction*: The teacher listens for misconceptions or understandings expressed as students work together. *Fairness, equity* for all students and respect for diversity: The teacher demonstrates that each student's uniqueness is valued by describing how the differentiated goals, instruction, and assessments meet students' needs. Examples include:
- Providing preferential seating and appropriate assistance.
- Recognizing learning styles, cultural values, and examples of fair play.
- Giving all students the opportunity to roll cars down ramps of different heights.
- Explaining why students are grouped in a certain way; why the student in the blue shirt uses a spelling device when writing or why only student A uses a particular tool or technology.
- Each member of the group has a role and is responsible for part of the activity.
- *Note:* In a 1:1 video, student-to-student interaction is impossible. Be sure it strongly shows in the other video.

Why These Work!

Making those elements evident in the video provides strong support and evidence and lends validity to the Written Commentary. They show support for the bullets in the *Selecting a Lesson for Each Video* section of your instructions. The video shows the *what* of a lesson, the writing explains the *why* of a lesson. It's a reasonable assumption that if the lesson is well planned—for both content and the evidence assessors expect to see—you stand a better chance of creating a segment *that works* without exhausting yourself and your students by filming over and over. You still may need several filming attempts, but you increase the odds that you won't be trying to get a usable video segment at the last minute or in a panic.

Because the standards are embedded within the prompts, the video segments that include as much evidence as possible may be ones that will work. The purpose of the video is to *support* the Written Commentary, so the assessors read the component, watch the video, then read the component again to verify the meshing of the two.

Demonstrating the Standards

At the beginning of each component is a list of Standards that are significant to that component. At each planning step, ask what could occur in the video to show that Standard? For example:

- When students are engaged in a discussion that deepens their understanding, what standard is evident?
- When students interact with each other, what standard is evident?
- When students are able to make choices, what standard is evident?

Often more than one Standard can be evidenced. The Standards contain multiple examples to help you plan and recognize examples in your own practice.

Looking for Clues in the NB Standards, Instructions, Prompts, and Rubric

Reading the component instructions thoroughly is the best way to identify evidence that assessors expect to see. It's also important to be familiar with the Level 4 Rubric, which explains the 3Cs: *clear, consistent, convincing* evidence. Specific examples of evidence are included in the explanation of each Standard, and incorporating your own specific examples makes a stronger case for your accomplished teaching. Reading the Standards and highlighting specific strategies that are *appropriate for your students, at this time, in this setting* will move you in the right direction. These contain clues about the types of evidence key to each component. For example:

- If a prompt asks for *specific evidence of approaches, strategies, techniques, or activities shown in the video*, be sure to include several examples from your practice in your writing. General responses are not strong evidence. Be specific.
- Use the key words from the prompt to point to specific examples from the video.

What Does Evidence in a Video Look Like?

- Here are some places to look and listen for evidence in a video. Pay attention to:
    - What is said
    - What is done
    - What questions are asked
    - Facial expressions
    - Body language
    - Level of engagement
    - Interactions
    - Instructional Materials
    - Goals and Objectives
    - Strategies
    - Assessments

Each of the above is connected to one or more of the Five Core Propositions and hence to one or more Standards. If assessors see the above evidence in your video, and if you write about the evidence with specific examples, you will produce a strong component.

What Works! Be Specific!

Citing *specific examples* of the above evidence is the best way to provide the clear, consistent, and convincing evidence called for in the Level 4 Rubric. The key word is *specific*! Following are some *hypothetical* examples:

- Because I knew that Todd struggled to find the area of a quadrilateral, I gave him a set of centimeter cubes to practice filling the interior spaces of square and rectangular shapes. At the beginning of the video, he uses the cubes to fill the shapes (find the area). Next he draws his own squares on graph paper. At the end of the video, he explains the process to his partner. This showed me he was gaining understanding the concept of *area* so he could soon apply the formula to quadrilaterals.
- The girl in the red sweater repeatedly insisted that insects had eight legs, so I matched her with a compatible partner to read *The Wonderful World of Insects* together. Later in the video, she correctly draws an insect with six legs.
- Group 3 made several unsuccessful attempts to assemble the model. They argued, so I approached and asked what procedure they had followed so far. I asked the group to come up with a strategy that would help them assemble the model without missing any steps. Their solution was to ask Group 4 to show them the steps they had used to complete the model. While watching Group 4, Richard realized they had not matched the parts correctly and pointed this out to his partners. As a result, Group 3 was able to return to their model and complete it successfully.

Why These Work!

Specific examples are where strong evidence is found. Evidence = Examples

Using the Leveled Scoring Rubrics: An Underused Resource:

At the end of Component 3, after the forms, are the Leveled Rubrics. These are what the Assessors have beside them as they score. If they use them, so should you. They should be within sight as you write the Written Commentaries. You'll aim to address the Level 4 Rubric, but you should be informed of the differences in each level. How is a Level 3 response different than a Level 4 or Level 2? I encourage you to pay particular attention to the Level 2 rubric statements and and how they differ from the Level 3 statement. I encourage you to do that because scores on the 2 level are the most common. Scores of 2 aren't awful, but they also aren't great. One can certify with some 2s, but not with all 2s . . . so analyzing the level different levels can make a difference. Each level has nuanced terms and language used to describe performance.

- Level 4: Performance provides *clear, consistent, and convincing* evidence and contains many specific examples and well-explained rationales.
- Level 3: Performance provides *clear* evidence. Consistent and convincing evidence may be present, but not strong. There are some rationales and examples but they may lack specificity.
- Level 2: Performance provides limited evidence; there is general evidence but lacks convincing evidence such as specific rationales and examples. Writing is too general and may not be consistently clear.
- Level 1: Performance provides *little or no* evidence. Evidence is sparse, weak, too general, or missing.
- *Clear:* Anyone can read the work and understand it.
- *Consistent* means the writing makes sense, numbers add up and there are no contradictions. Something mentioned one place may surface again—like a thread woven through a tapestry.
- *Convincing:* You've given specific, detailed, appropriate examples and rationales. Evidence supports the "claims" made in the writing.

What Works!

Studying all levels of the rubrics gives you a roadmap to follow as you plan and begin writing.

Why This Works!

The rubrics are your blueprint for including evidence in your writing and showing the NB Standards in your writing.

Choosing the Video Segment:

- Read the instructions so you are crystal clear about the requirements regarding time, grouping, number of segments, and editing, for example. Directions must be followed exactly. They are the final word.
- Know the *maximum* number of minutes specified in the instructions.
- A segment can be slightly *shorter* than the maximum number of minutes allowed.
- Follow the *20% Rule*: a video should not be more than 20 percent shorter than the maximum minutes allowed. Thus, a video with a fifteen minutes maximum should probably not be shorter than 12 minutes. This is not an official NB rule, but is a good rule of thumb to apply.
- Watch the entire lesson once to get a sense of its quality. Then, once you have some promising footage, try these strategies to locate a usable segment:

Watch the Segment Multiple Times

- *Watch the first time* to verify that the *goal(s) is* evident and the activity supports that goal.
- *Watch the second time* with the sound off to watch for body language and facial expressions that indicate *student engagement and interactions*.
- *Watch the third time* with only sound (turn your back to the screen). Listen for *exchanges* between the teacher and students, students and the teacher, and student to student, as well as *discourse about the content*.
- *Watch the fourth time* with your class. The comments they make can be insightful! It's guaranteed that they'll notice things you didn't, and you can include these in the analysis and reflection sections.
- Watching the video with colleagues and other candidates is also an effective strategy.

Documenting the Standards in the Video

Review the video segment for evidence of the Standards listed in each component and in the Level 4 Rubric. Note the evidence (examples) you find.

- What did you do and say?
- What did the students do and say?
- What interactions took place between people?
- What interactions took place with the content?
- What did you do to promote a climate of learning?
- Are all of the sections in the component instructions addressed?
- Did you respond to *all parts* of the prompt and questions?
- Consider not using parts showing directions or transitions because they may lack evidence.

Let's return to the sample scenario described earlier to analyze which Standards might be demonstrated by the student-to-student interaction described. *The scenario: A class participates in a science inquiry activity with ramps. Each member is responsible for helping to determine the surface and height of their ramp. They have all received direct instruction and completed other activities to build foundational knowledge about force and motion. All will have opportunity to complete both activities.*

Using the Middle Childhood Generalist Certificate Standards, here are possible ways the Standards could be evidenced. Note the use of the first person to model the writing style. Using the first person assures that the teacher is visible within the lesson.

Establishing an Environment for Learning:

- I arranged groups to address student strengths/needs and assigned jobs within the group to address learning strengths, needs, interests, and language fluency.
- I presented instructions, materials, and activities that are age appropriate and foster organization and manage learning.

Knowledge of Content and Curriculum:

- I planned appropriate goals and objectives.
- The information I taught was accurate and connected to real life.
- I presented the core knowledge in a variety of ways.

Instructional Decision Making:

- The activity and product fostered inquiry and required students to explain their thinking.
- I provided a variety of non-fiction materials to foster reading skills and extend and enrich learning.
- I asked students to demonstrate ways the topic applies to real life.
- I gave students choices in how they constructed their ramps.

Respect for Diversity:

- I planned activities to address various learning styles and students' strengths.
- I planned activities that appeal to both males and females.

Reflection:

- I analyzed the results of the assessments in order to know whether instruction was successful and decided where to go next.
- I realized I needed to re-teach Newton's Laws because students had not yet corrected misconceptions.

The above points are examples of how to address and write about the Standards your component emphasizes in the Written Commentary and on the Forms. Note as well, how the Standards connect to the Architecture of Accomplished Teaching.

Finalizing the Details

- Select a segment that demonstrates the *most* evidentiary support and is the richest with the Standards and Level 4 Rubric evidence.

- Find a segment that fits the time frame in the instructions.
- Use a stopwatch or the time print on the video for exact times.
- Note the standards evidenced.
- List the specific examples you can use as evidence.
- Follow formatting and directions found within the instructions and on the Electronic Submission at a Glance page exactly!
- Call 1-800-22TEACH with questions. Rely only on your instructions and/or the NBPTS for information!

Writing the Video Component: Describe, Analyze, and Reflect

In the current version of the process, all certificate areas respond to the same set of prompts, with just a minor variation or two. This creates a more even playing field from certificate to certificate. You use this set of prompts for *both* videos. Follow *your* certificate area prompts, even if a colleagues' differs.

Every component requires three types of writing: description, analysis, and reflection, and each prompt can call for one or more of the three types of writing. The borders between the types can be fuzzy, but keep the following generalities in mind:

- *Description* is an objective retelling to give the reader a sense of being in the classroom. It answers the questions *what* and *which*. Key verbs are *describe, state, list, and define*.
- *Analysis* reveals the thought processes used to make instructional decisions and explains the significance and impact of the evidence submitted. Analysis involves the interpretation of the facts. Key analysis questions are *why, how,* and *so what*. Key verbs are *analyze, explain, because, in order to,* and *interpret*.
- *Reflection* deals with the thought processes that occur after a teaching situation. It is hindsight and takes place in order to improve future teaching practices. The key reflection question now what? Reflection cues include improve, change, and in the future.
- *The climate in the classroom:* how factors such as the nature of the learning experience, the degree of intellectual risk-taking encouraged

by the teacher, respect, fairness, equity, access, and classroom management come together.

- *Student engagement with the content:* the extent to which the students are actively involved in the learning.
- *Interactions:* verbal and non-verbal interactions between the teacher and students, the students and the teacher, and student to student.
- *Discourse Environment:* the nature of the discussion which occurs, the role of the teacher in promoting inquiry and debate, and the student responses.

What Works! Writing about the Video

- The video itself isn't scored separately, but it's vital to support the Written Commentary.
- Point out your teaching behaviors. Some, such as questioning strategies, are obvious, while others, like using an attention signal or a tap on a desk are more subtle.
- Refer to specific moments and explain what you were thinking when you said a particular thing or took a particular action. Even if an action is obvious, explaining the rationale behind it will make the writing more convincing.
- Describe any adjustments you made during the lesson and tell why.
- Point out any AHA! moments that occur in student understanding.
- You can refer to students using an identifying characteristic, that is, *the blond boy.*
- You can use a time reference if you have space and feel it will help the assessors find the evidence. It's optional. *At 7:54, Mike was able to borrow successfully when he subtracted.*
- If it is difficult to hear something important, you can script the dialogue: *"When the volcano erupted, the boy in the red shirt said, "The liquid spurting out is magma."* This highlights specific evidence.
- Call attention to student engagement. Remember to include the more subtle signs such as eye contact, body language, posture, and taking notes. Engagement doesn't always have to be active movement or talk.

- If a student's behavior is problematic, don't discard a video for that reason alone. It may allow you to discuss challenges you deal with (possibly also mentioned in the Instructional Context) and your rationale for addressing the behavior.
- Use *specific examples* from the video. Make this your mantra!

Component 3: Forms and Materials

Component 3 has three forms. Download forms and type responses within the brackets. Always follow the directions in the gray boxes.

- *Introduction to Entry Form:* This form gives a general overview of the entire entry then shares the focus of EACH of the two videos. You complete this form *once*.
- *Instructional Context Sheet:* This form is about your teaching context: your classes, your courses, your grade level(s), and your students. Some questions parallel prompts in the Component 2 Instructional Context. You complete this form for *each video*. That means you'll fill this form *twice*. Some of all information may be the same on each form depending on the class(es) you use.
- *Instructional Planning Form:* This form is where you list *each* lesson's goals and instructional format. You also describe the *instructional materials* used in the lesson. These may include: Anything you used to *teach* the lesson: charts, manipulatives, graphic organizers, props, texts, models, and much more. These can be scanned copies of the item or a photo.
- A lesson plan showing the entire lesson can be an instructional material.
- This is also where you list any edits that appear. You fill this form out for *each* video—hence you'll do it *twice*. There are some special, important directions in the *Gray Box* of this form. It is with this form that you attach the 2-page *Writing About Planning* section. Don't forget this instruction. Component 3 cannot receive an accomplished score if the *Writing About Planning* is not submitted.

Writing about Planning Section: Don't Forget It!

Page 6 in the Component 3 instructions holds an important section. The prompts in this section pertain to planning your video lessons. You respond to the prompts for *each* video. That means you will answer them *twice*. This is meant to be completed *before* making the videos. You know this because the verbs are written in the present, not past tense. You attach these responses to each *Instructional Planning Form* you complete.

Electronic Submission at a Glance: Your Component 3 Checklist:

This chart is your Component 3 checklist of exactly what to submit: types and number of files, response lengths, and many additional specific details. This is an underused resource. Let this be your ultimate guide to all that is to be submitted. Check off each item as you upload and submit your work.

Why These Work!

Presenting evidence in the videos is not about looking a particular way, sounding a particular way, or teaching a particular way. The video is not meant to be a "Hollywood production." It is about showing your teaching practice in an honest way; giving a snapshot of what you really do and how you really teach. It's about how you plan, how you respond, and how you impact student learning using your own teaching style, your understanding of your students, your knowledge of content, and your pedagogical skills.

Component 4
Effective and Reflective Practitioner

You know you are a National Board candidate when: You get so comfortable filming that you confuse your classroom with the set of a reality show and make side comments to the camera.

Overview

Are you planning to tackle C4 this school year? Component 4 focuses on your ability to use reflection to effectively develop knowledge of your students (KOS) and apply that knowledge to assessment practices to move their learning forward. You'll gather information/data from a variety of sources and collaborate with colleagues and the larger community to impact your students' learning. The data you submit, the sources of that information, and how you use it will be specific to your subject area and the unique characteristics of the students you teach, school, district, and community.

Component 4 also directly addresses NB Standards not addressed in other components. The titles of these Standards vary by certificate area, but they address advancing professionalism, professional development, collaboration, and leadership.

What Do You Need to Do?

Component 4 asks you to focus on your knowledge of students, use of assessments, collaboration, professional development, and participation in learning communities. You will:

- *Collect* relevant information from families/caregivers, the larger community, colleagues, and other sources to describe and build a profile of a group of students.

- *Choose* assessments based on your knowledge of students gathered from collaborations and multiple sources, the learning objectives of the unit you teach, and your understanding of sound assessment principles and practices. You will focus on formative, summative, and student self-assessment.
- *Analyze* your assessment practices to explain how they have a positive impact on student learning.
- *Reflect* on the effectiveness of your assessment practices to improve student learning.
- *Submit* examples of assessments and data used for formative and summative purposes.
- *Provide* evidence that you use assessment data to positively impact student learning.

What Works!

Tightly connect the information/data in the Knowledge of Students section with the data in the Generation and Use of Assessment section. These sections go hand in hand.

Why This Works!

Your knowledge of Students is the *foundation* for all your decisions and choices in the Assessment section. Those connections must be visible to the assessors.

Component 4: Collecting and Using Data: Your Component 4 Roadmap

C4 is often described as the *assessment component*, but actually, this component is about *data* and how you *use* the data you collect from a variety of sources and assessments. In each part of the component, the assessor should see the following cycle repeated:

1. You *collect* meaningful data from a variety of valid sources.
2. You *analyze* the data to identify trends/outliers, etc.
3. You *use* that data analysis to take an action(s), for example, design or re-design instruction, tweak your unit exam, choose professional development, initiate collaboration etc.
4. Then you *gather* data on how well it worked and begin the cycle again.

The Four Sections/Chunks of Component 4

Component 4 is divided into four sections/chunks that make up your Written Commentary and the evidence you'll submit. Because of this, it can feel disjointed, less cohesive than other components that have a tighter focus. These elements are:

1. Knowledge of Students
2. Generation and Use of Assessment Data
3. Participation in Learning Communities

    Professional Learning Need

    Student Need

4. Reflection

Section 1: Knowledge of Students (KOS) and Profile Group

The Knowledge of Students (KOS) Section may be the single most important section in all of Component 4 because it is the foundation upon which the other sections are built, particularly Section 2, Generation and Use of Assessment. It is the section candidates have the most difficulty writing. In the Knowledge of Students section, you gather information/data about your Profile Group of students—the students to whom you will teach a unit of study and assess learning.

Start collecting student data EARLY—as soon as your school year begins. If starting C4 later in the year, just dig in and start researching and collecting.

Look at the C4 instructions for Knowledge of Students and think about how you can use beginning-of-year surveys, data from various sources, and your own observations during first few weeks of class to produce evidence of your KOS (Knowledge of Students.)

Creating the Group Profile

The Group Profile is a description of the group of students you teach and will feature in the Assessment section of Component 4. The Profile helps the assessors *see* the students as learners.

- In most certificate areas, the group will be a whole class, but could be another configuration such as a pull-out or a needs-based group. See your specific instructions as this varies from certificate to certificate.
- ENS Certificate: Students must have an IEP and/or be identified as gifted.
- Literacy, School Counseling, English as a New Language, and Career and Technical Education certificates state that a group can be *students you work with separately, but who share similar needs and/or characteristics* (EX: same language of origin). You would group them together into one Profile Group. Check your instructions!
- Students must be your *current* students (*this* school year) or your students within the 12 months preceding your submission (12 months *before* the submission date).
- Fifty-one percent of the students must be within the stated age range for your certificate *during the period you collect evidence*. Refer to your certificate-specific NB Standards for a complete discussion of this topic and to see specific examples.
- Use multiple sources to gather information/data:
  - Assessment data.
  - School data from previous years.
  - Observational data.
  - Surveys from families/caregivers.
  - School personnel.
  - Professionals in the field.
  - Colleagues.

- Community resources that may affect the school and/or students you teach.

Show in your writing that you've used *at least two* of the following:

- Families
- Colleagues
- Professionals in the district or in the field
- Other community members (after school care, social workers, etc.)

Specific information, data, and/or evidence can be gathered from:

- Progress Charting
- Emails: Print and save
- Ongoing/Anecdotal Notes
- Surveys
- Communication Log: Phone calls, notes, conferences, etc. Track the dates, reasons for the contacts, and outcomes.
- Other appropriate methods of sharing information. This is not an exhaustive list.

The wise candidate will begin collecting information for the Profile Group, based on Knowledge of Students at the beginning of the school year. Find an organizational strategy for keeping track of what will become a large volume of evidence/data over time. Create files or folders, throw everything into one or more boxes, stuff envelopes . . . whatever method works for you. Use the *KISS* system: **K**eep **I**t **S**uper **S**imple!

What Works!

Begin Component 4 immediately when school starts. Have I said this before? There is much evidence/data to collect and many forms to fill out. However, if starting later, gather the KOS evidence as quickly as possible.

Why This Works!

Give yourself the gift of time to plan, teach, reflect, collect evidence/data, and write.

Section 2: Generation and Use of Assessment Data

The Knowledge of Students and Generation and Use of Assessment sections of Component 4 combine to make up the largest parts of the writing and evidence you'll submit for Component 4. Seven of the fourteen pages of the Written Commentary are allocated to these two sections, so they are important and will impact one's score. You will plan a unit of study and learning objectives for the students in your Profile Group that provides opportunities to use both *formative and summative* assessments *and the data they generate* in ways that are meaningful within the context of the instructional unit. To be meaningful, an assessment must:

- Be appropriate for the students in the Profile Group, meaning it fits the age/developmental range of the students and assesses the objectives you taught.
- Assess the actual learning goals/objectives.
- Produce results/data that are accurate and reliable.
- Produce information/data that contributes to student learning.
- Produce data to inform your future instruction.

What Will You Do?

You will teach a unit of study within your certificate area subject matter.

- *Choose* a unit within the subjects/topics covered in your certificate area that allows you to give the three required types of assessments.
- *Choose a unit* long enough to allow opportunity for the three types of assessments, yet of a manageable length. A semester or year-long unit/topic could be unwieldy. There is no required length time for the unit.
- You'll submit information/data and materials connected with *one formative, one summative, and three student self-assessments*. For each, you'll feature either a teacher-created or a ready-made assessment of your choice.
- You can *give* any assessment you want—including a copyrighted one, but cannot *submit any assessment* that is in whole or part copyrighted or test secure.
- If you *give* a copyrighted assessment, you will *describe* it on a form rather than *submit* it.

- *Research* Formative, Summative, and Student Self-Assessment if you are unclear about any aspect of them including the timing of them and their purpose.
- *Research* Student Self-Assessments and teach students how to take them. Yes, even three year olds can self-assess in meaningful ways.

Formative Assessments (FA):

Formative assessments are a range of formal and informal assessments conducted by teachers *during the learning process* in order to inform instruction, and/or modify teaching and learning activities to improve student learning. The words "during instruction" is critical.

- For Component 4 purposes, the timing of the Formative Assessment is crucial. The operative word is DURING instruction; not *before* any instruction, not *after* instruction is completed—*DURING instruction!* I cannot emphasize this enough.
- Formative assessments are used to provide feedback data to students and inform instruction.
- They are generally not graded (but can be) and are considered part of the learning process.
- They are usually short, quick, and focused. Examples may include:
- Observation
- Running Records
- Quick Writes
- Warm-up Problems
- Games
- Ticket out of Class/Exit Slips
- Discussion
- Graphic Organizers
- Individual Responses on Whiteboards, Clickers, etc.
- Peer/Self Assessments
- Think - Pair - Share
- Summaries/Reflections
- Curriculum-Provided quizzes

There are many resources in books and the internet, available with lists and descriptions of specific activities. "Google" *formative assessments* and you'll find dozens of ideas.

Formative Assessment in a Nutshell:

- The Formative Assessment is given *during* the unit—while you are teaching it—*after* some instruction, over *part* of the unit objectives—the ones you've taught up to that point.
- Many give the Formative Assessment and Student Self-Assessments at about the half-way point in the unit but exactly when is your choice.
- The Formative Assessment produces data that you use to inform your future instruction
- The Student Self-Assessment covers approximately the same objectives as the Formative Assessment and is given at about the same time. *They should be connected.* You use data from both of these assessments, *together*, to inform your instruction from that point forward.
- You can *give* multiple Formative Assessments if you want, but you'll *submit only one.*
- The *surest* choice is to connect the Formative Assessment and the Student Self-Assessment.
- The Student Self-Assessment *can* be given after the Summative Assessment, but if you do that, be sure it informs future instruction *connected to the unit featured in Component 4*—which can be tricky.
- The Summative Assessment covers all the objectives of the unit and is given at the end of instruction.

Summative Assessments (SA):

The goal of a summative assessment is to evaluate student learning at the *end of an instructional sequence/unit* by comparing it against some standard or benchmark. Summative assessments are often are higher stakes, meaning they have a high point value. They assess cumulative knowledge used to measure student growth. They usually result in a grade/score/data used to evaluate the learning that has taken place. Examples of summative assessments might be:

- Mid-term Exams
- End-of-Term Assessments
- Final Projects
- District Benchmark Tests
- Curriculum-Provided Assessments
- State-Mandated Assessments
- Scores used for accountability for schools (AYP) and students (report card grades)..
- Term Papers
- Portfolios
- Projects
- Performances/Demonstrations
- Checklists (especially for younger students)

More about Formative Assessment: The Pre-test/Post-test Dilemma

For my NB work, are pretests formative assessments? If the exact same assessment is used as a pre- and post-test, have you given a formative and a summative assessment? These are questions candidates grapple with when planning assessments.

It's generally agreed that pre-tests *are* a type of formative assessment because they help identify students' current level of knowledge of a subject, and their skill sets and capabilities. Knowing students' strengths and weaknesses at the outset of instruction, as measured by a pretest can inform your instruction to help you better plan what unit to teach and how to teach it.

However, the Formative Assessment the National Board asks you to *submit* measures student progress *along the way* and provides feedback and information *during* the instructional process while learning is taking place. Formative assessments you *submit* guide instructional changes *during* the unit. Pre- and post-tests can certainly inform instruction and measure learning. Considering the accepted *timing* of formative assessments, *during* instruction rather than *before* instruction, a pre-test may not be the best choice to submit for a formative assessment. It's generally accepted that a post-test is synonymous with summative assessment because it measures cumulative learning after instruction.

Three Formative Assessment Takeaways:

1. The Formative Assessment you *submit* must be given *during the* instruction of the unit.
2. You may *give* more than one Formative Assessment, but will *submit only one*.
3. *Give* a pre-test if you want, before instruction, and use it as you always do, but do not *submit* a pre-test as your example of a Formative Assessment.

Student Self-Assessments (SSAs)

You'll also include *three student self-assessments*. Information in the GENERAL Portfolio Instructions state you may submit these with *either* the Formative *or* the Summative Assessment, *but not both*. If a candidate submits self-assessments for both types, only the ones submitted for the Formative Assessment will be scored. This *may imply* that self-assessment *during* the learning process is more highly valued than a summative self-evaluation. Think about *why* that may be:

Purposes of Student Self-Assessment:

- Self-Assessment encourages students to reflect on their learning experiences.
- They develop student experiences with rubrics, reflective questions, and/or graphic organizers.
- They allow teachers to tap into student thinking and differences in order to see how our teaching can respond to their needs.
- Students gain experience evaluating their own work to improve performance.

The evaluation target must align with the goals/objectives of the learning. Examples of self-assessment might include:

- Rubrics that clarify what level of work will earn a particular score.
- Three Things I Learned . . .
- Graphic Organizers.
- Ticket Out of Class.
- Teacher-Student Conference.
- Checklists.
- Individual Student Interviews (usually with younger children).

When choosing the assessment to submit, there are many factors to consider:

- The Unit Plan.
- The Unit Objectives.
- Why the assessments are appropriate for these students, at this time, in this place.
- How directly do the assessments evaluate the unit objectives.

You'll also need to think about:

- The purpose of the assessment.
- How it aligns with the learning objectives.
- How the results/data support your teaching practice and inform your instruction.
- How and why the assessment was developed or selected.
- How it was administered and scored.
- How the results/data are intended to be used.

What Works!

Using Formative and Summative assessments helps you accumulate a well-rounded picture of student learning. Using assessment data to inform your teaching means you analyze and interpret data, then use that data to confirm and/or modify teaching strategies to improve student learning. This combination of assessments and the analysis and thinking required to use the data appropriately has a powerful impact on teaching and learning.

Why This Works!

Having a toolbox of assessment strategies generates data you can use to inform your teaching. The more you know about your students and how they learn, the more effective your teaching can be.

Assessment Data Takeaways:

The assessments given in the Generation and Use of Assessment section are very important. They contribute heavily to the Component 4 score. For the most impact, be sure the Formative Assessment you submit conforms to the National Board definition and timing requirements.

Connecting the Sections:

The Knowledge of Students section and the Generation and Use of Assessment section must be tightly connected. You must incorporate what you learned from the Knowledge of Students sources in the unit you teach and its assessments. Study the graphics and other C4 information in the Appendix.

Section 3: Participation in Learning Communities:

The National Board uses Learning Communities in a broad context. Generally speaking, in an educational setting, a learning community is a group of people who share common academic goals and attitudes and who meet at least semi-regularly to collaborate to improve teaching and the academic performance of students. Many school faculties use this type of small-group collaboration as a form of professional development and use the term *Professional Learning Communities*. Educators, often grade-level teams, same-subject teachers, or departments come together to share expertise, interpret, and share data, and set teaching and learning goals.

Learning Communities can extend beyond the school walls. For example, candidates may interact with Learning Communities within their district, community, or Professional Association. Learning Communities can take various forms and purposes. Here are some possibilities:

- National/Professional Organizations
- Online groups, blogs, or discussion boards

- Pedagogical PLC
- Grade Level PLC
- Book study group
- "Pick-up" PLC—an informal group, may be a committee that chooses a topic for study and discussion. Example: How to create effective rubrics; Share/design/use the product/collect data
- Learning communities within a District, Community, Professional Association, or even digitally across the country/world

You'll include information, data, and evidence of your involvement in learning communities. You'll describe, analyze, and reflect on how your participation is relevant to you and how it impacts both the students you teach and your teaching practice. You'll explain ways your participation in learning community impacts how you gather information to inform your instructional and assessment practices and contributes to positive, effective learning changes for your students.

The Professional Learning Need (PLN):

The Professional Learning Need addresses something you need to LEARN better in order to TEACH something better. The Professional Learning Need is defined as a need for professional learning for yourself and/or your colleagues that you identified *as a result of your knowledge of students* (either a particular group or a broader population) and assessment practices. This need could be cumulative over time.

What Will You Do?:

- *Identify* a need.
- *Explain* how you addressed the need.
- *Tell* the impact of your efforts on student learning using data you gathered.
- *Ask* yourself: What do I need to *learn* in order to teach something better?
- *Determine* if this is a need only *you* have, OR a need *you* had and learned about and now can share with colleagues who also have this same need to learn.

- *Use* data from your knowledge of Students to determine the need. How do you know your students have particular "needs" so that you know you need to address them?
- *Determine* if the group of students you use will be the same as your Profile Group or another group—even a whole grade level, department, or school.
- *Decide if* the need will be *academic, behavioral, SEL* etc.
- *Decide* if Professional Development may play a role. What workshops, training, personal studies, online activities, book clubs etc. have you participated in over the last 2 years in order to learn something so you could teach it better?
- *Determine* if the Professional Development is something just YOU need(ed) to learn for your own class(es) OR something wider such as departmental / school-wide offered or required by your district—trainings pertaining to programs you are expected to learn and implement for your students. Examples: LETRS, Science of Reading, SEL/TRAUMA trainings, etc.
- *Document* how you used *your learning* not only to impact *your* students' learning but also how you *shared* your learning so colleagues could learn and impact *their* students' learning. You would collect data (testimonials) from other teachers about how *they* used this learning to impact *their* students. This "sharing with colleagues" part is OPTIONAL.
- *Focus* the evidence for the PLN on evidence of your learning.
- Think: notes taken during PD that show your learning, lesson plan incorporating new learning, PD agenda showing topics studied, meeting notes etc.
- *Use* strong evidence/data. Certificates of Attendance are not considered strong evidence because they don't actually show what was learned—only what was attended.
- *Ensure* evidence/data submitted for the Professional Learning Need is *different* than evidence submitted for any other section. Evidence/data should not overlap—especially for the impact on student learning part.
- The Professional Learning Need MAY be connected to any of the other parts (Assessment section, Student Need). It CAN be connected BUT may also stand alone.

- Consider using *before/after* data. The *before* data might highlight the need for more learning on your part, and the *after* data would show the impact on student learning.

The Student Need:

Here, you shift gears and focus on how you used *advocacy, collaboration, and/or leadership* to address a student need. Notice the *and/or* language.

What Will You Do?

- *Identify* a need.
- *Explain* how you addressed the need.
- *Collect* data on collaboration, advocacy, and/or leadership and the impact on student learning.
- *Tell* the impact of your efforts on student learning.
- *Use* your knowledge of students to determine the need.
- *Decide* if the need will be academic, behavioral, SEL etc.
- *Plan* ways to *collaborate with others, advocate, or show leadership* in some way to address the need. Examples:
    - *Collaborate*: You work with the school counselor to ___.
    - *Advocate*: You work with the PTA or write a GRANT to obtain funds for student ___.
    - *Leadership*: You recognized a need for __ at your school and worked with a committee and others to provide ___.

Collaboration, advocacy, and leadership often overlap when addressing the student need.

- *Understand* the Student Need applies to *groups, not individual students*. The group could be your Profile Group, another class (or set of classes), a grade level, department, whole school, or even a sub-set of some kind such as gifted students or students in the twenty-fifth percentile or lower etc.
- *Follow* the same timeframe as the Professional Learning Need for evidence collection and evidence of student learning.

- *Use evidence/data* for the Student Need that focuses on *collaboration, advocacy, and/or leadership*.
- *Think*: emails with others, schedule/agenda of meetings with others, notes taken at meetings etc.
- *Consider* using *before/after* data. The *before* data might highlight the need for collaboration, advocacy, and/or leadership, and the *after* data would show the impact the collaboration, advocacy, and/or leadership had on student learning.
- *Use* evidence for the Student Need that is different than evidence you've used for any other section, especially different than for the impact on Student Learning part of the Professional Learning Need.

Professional Learning Need and Student Need Pitfalls:

Component 4 can feel very big and disjointed. This leads to some unique issues that impact scores. Assessors have shared three main issues with this section of C4:

- Candidates fail to plan ahead for the Professional Learning Need and Student Need parts. They wait until spring, then realize they don't have the PD needed or strong evidence to submit. The Professional Learning Need and the Student Need can benefit from collecting before/after evidence. By not planning ahead, the window for collecting such evidence is cut short.
- Candidates either omit writing about the impact on student learning, or write weakly about it—showing little evidence/data. Don't neglect that prompt. Collect evidence as you go along.
- Candidates use the same evidence, especially evidence pertaining to the impact on student learning for both parts. The needs are different and the evidence of impact on student learning must also be different.
- Candidates use only one student for the Student Need section when it's meant to address a group or subset of students.
- The evidence/data submitted does not strongly connect to the needs or support the claims made in the writing.

It is imperative to read the C4 directions for this section *multiple* times. Make yourself lists, outlines, charts, etc. to keep it all straight in your head. This *nutshell* does not contain all you need to know about this section. Pour over the directions. Careful planning will make the Professional Learning Need and Student Need parts go smoother.

The Reflection Section:

Reflection is a special type of *analysis* where one looks back in order to look forward. *Analysis* is the most evidentiary of the three types of writing. The responses to the reflection prompts contain strong evidence, so even though you may be tired by the time this section comes along, don't skimp on the reflection. There is room for many specific details and examples as well as rationales.

Connecting the Sections:

- The Knowledge of Students and Generation and Use of Assessment sections MUST connect with each other.
- The Professional Learning Need MAY connect to the Assessment section OR *stand alone*.
- The Professional Learning Need MAY connect to the Student Need section OR *stand alone*.
- The Student Need section MAY connect to the Assessment section OR stand *alone*.
- The Student Need section MAY connect to the Professional Learning Need OR stand *alone*.

Study the graphics in the Appendix for more visual examples of how the sections MAY and MUST be connected.

Unpacking the Component 4 Prompts:

Understanding the prompts can be challenging. Some are long, have multiple parts, and use terminology that tests one's vocabulary. The following might help you get to the central ideas of the prompts, Some good old-fashioned parsing of the prompts can be enlightening. Some, especially in the Knowledge of Students section begin with nouns—those will need mostly descriptive writing. Many prompts in the Assessment and Participation in Learning Communities ask What or How, which indicates a mix of description and analysis. Prompts in the Reflection Section ask you to look back in order to look ahead, which is a special kind of analysis. As you respond to the prompts, add rationales as often possible to strengthen your writing. And always be specific with specific examples.

Focus on Knowledge of Students Prompts:

- Information/data about the Profile Group.
- Sources for information/data gathered.
- Rationale for using those sources.
- Trends you identified from the information gathered.
- Factors you took into account when analyzing and reflecting on your sources.
- Needs of the Profile Group.
- The support you provided.
- How you collaborated to meet those needs.

Focus of Generation and Use of Assessment Data Prompts:

- How your knowledge of the Profile Group informed the assessments you used.
- How you used data to modify assessment(s) to meet students' needs.
- How the results showed consistent, fair, and accurate information/data about student learning.
- How the analysis of the formative assessment data gave you information about the group's learning of the unit objectives.
- What patterns, trends, or outliers were evident in the assessment results?
- What adjustments, if any, were made to the unit plan you made based on data from the formative assessment.
- What resources/supports you provided with regard to collaboration.
- What analysis of the summative assessment results/data told you about the group's learning of the unit objectives.
- How the summative assessment data informed future instruction.
- How you provided opportunities for feedback/self-assessment during the unit of study,

- How you applied the knowledge you acquired from various sources and the assessment data to future instruction with this group of students.

Focus on Participation in Learning Communities Prompts:

- How you identified a professional learning need.
- Factors you considered to meet that need.
- How you identified the student need requiring advocacy, collaboration, and/or leadership.
- Who you worked with and what your role.
- Factors or information you considered to determine how to meet that need.
- How your learning and/or collaboration, advocacy, and/or leadership impacted student learning.

Focus of Reflection Prompts:

- Effectiveness of your efforts to gain knowledge of the Profile Group.
- Approaches or additional steps you might take in the future to deepen that knowledge.
- How your assessment practices have evolved; how you have learned from your experiences, collaboration with colleagues, families/care-givers, community members, and participation in learning communities.
- How your expectations of professional learning and collaborative learning community activities regarding student learning and growth were met or not met.
- How do you plan to continue to have a positive impact on student learning and growth in the future, considering the major areas of professional practice addressed in Component 4.

E-Submission at a Glance:

This chart, found at the end of the Component 4 instructions, is your checklist of everything to be submitted. For each Component 4 section, it lists:

- What to Submit
- File Types
- Number of Files to be Submitted and Response Length
- Additional Information

Let this be your ultimate guide to all that is to be submitted. Check off each item as you upload and submit your work.

Component 4 Evidence/Data:

The evidence/data you select should match up with and support what you have discussed in the Written Commentary and on the Forms. In my discussion of the various sections, I've given lists of possible sources of evidence/data which can guide you towards selecting strong types of evidence/data. You always want to choose evidence/data that shows as much evidence as possible. Examples: Which shows more evidence?

- An email about choosing dates to meet to collaborate on the Student Need OR An email that shows a summary of the topics you discussed with someone you're collaborating with?
- A blank worksheet OR one filled out with student work/responses?
- A certificate of completion for a PD you used for the Professional Learning Need OR a lesson plan showing how you incorporated new learning into your planning?

Here are more examples of evidence/data samples you might use. The list is not exhaustive.

- Charts
- Graphs
- Spreadsheets (can be partial pages)
- Rubrics
- Running record examples
- PD syllabus
- Lesson Plan
- Before/after data (especially for the Professional Learning Need and Student Need)

- Meeting/Training Notes
- Contact Sheet/Communication Log
- Assessment Data
- Notes/letters from colleagues telling impact on student learning
- Screenshots
- Surveys (full or partial)
- Parent communications
- Photos (projects, etc.)
- Student work samples (complete or partial)
- If the Professional Learning Need and the Student Need are connected, you must use DIFFERENT evidence for each. The PLN evidence will focus on your learning and how it impacted student learning. The SN evidence will focus on the collaboration, advocacy, and/or leadership and how it impacted student learning.

Component 4 Forms:

Component 4 has more forms than any other component—7 Forms. Each describes, clarifies, or adds information to your writing in the Written Commentary. It's important each form be filled out completely and adhere to page limits. First, download the forms onto your computer from the zip file. Now you can type directly onto each form. The formats—font, size, margins and so on are automatically set—no worries there. The forms are not scored separately. They are part of the holistic scoring of the entire component, but a missing form can impact the score, so be thorough. *Pay special attention to the gray boxes on the forms. Do not delete or alter anything on any form.*

1. *Contextual Information Sheet:* This serves the same purpose as the Instructional Context section of Component 2. It is about the *class*.
2. *Group Information and Profile Form*: Promote 1 asks you to *describe information* you collected about the Profile Group students. Prompt 2 asks you to *describe the students* based on the information you collected.
3. *Instructional Context Form:* This form is about the unit you teach, the unit's objectives, and the rationale behind the assessments you used.

4. *Formative Assessment Materials Form:* Here you discuss the formative assessments you gave and the context for the Student Self-Assessments. The first prompt has multiple parts.
5. *Summative Assessment Materials Form:* Describe the Summative Assessment. If your Summative Assessment is copyrighted, be sure to write a thorough description since you can't submit it and the assessors won't see the real thing.
6. *Description of a Professional Learning Need*: Prompt 1 is about the actual *need* you chose, and Prompt 2 describes the *evidence* you submit.
7. *Description of a Student Need Form*: In Prompt 1, you describe the actual *need* you chose. Prompt 2 asks you to describe the *evidence*.

Using the Leveled Scoring Rubrics: An Underused Resource:

At the end of Component 4, after the forms, are the Leveled Rubrics. These are what the assessors have beside them as they score. If they use them, so should you. They should be within sight as you write the Written Commentary. You'll aim to address the Level 4 Rubric, but you should be informed of the differences at each level. How is a Level 3 response different than a Level 4 or Level 2. I encourage you to pay particular attention to the Level 2 rubric statements and how they differ from the Level 3 statement. I encourage you to do that because scores on the two levels are the most common. Scores of two aren't awful, but they also aren't great. One can certify with some 2s, but not with all 2s . . . so analyzing the level different levels can make a difference.

Each level has nuanced terms and language used to describe performance.

- Level 4: Performance provides *clear, consistent, and convincing* evidence and contains many specific examples and well-explained rationales.
- Level 3: Performance provides *clear* evidence. Consistent and convincing evidence may be present, but not strong. There are some rationales and examples but they may lack specificity.
- Level 2: Performance provides limited evidence; there is general evidence but lacks convincing evidence such as specific rationales and examples. Writing is too general and may not be consistently clear.

- Level 1: Performance provides *little or no* evidence. Evidence is sparse, weak, too general, or missing.
- *Clear:* Anyone can read the work and understand it.
- *Consistent* means the writing makes sense, numbers add up and there are no contradictions. Something mentioned one place may surface again—like a thread woven through a tapestry.
- *Convincing:* You've given specific, detailed, appropriate examples and rationales. Evidence supports the "claims" made in the writing.

What Works!

Studying all levels of the rubrics gives you a roadmap to follow as you plan and begin writing.

Why This Works!

The rubrics are your blueprint for including evidence in your writing and showing the NB Standards in your writing.

The Key to Component 4:

Data, data, data - good data you can analyze to inform your instruction and impact student learning is the key to C4.

7 Scoring

The Scoring Process

The National Board scoring process is the Gold Standard for fair assessment. Components 2–4 are submitted in mid-May. The C1 assessment window ends in mid-June. Assessors are all working teachers, and many are still teaching until mid-June, so no scoring can occur until then.

All assessors undergo rigorous training before any scoring can start. Some applicants are weeded out. Assessors are quality-checked regularly DURING the scoring cycle to assure inter-rater reliability. The Selected Response items in C1 are machine-scored, but the Constructed Response items in Component 1, and Components 2, 3, and 4 cannot be machine scored. These require careful human examination.

Once the scoring teams are set, components are scored from mid/late-June through August. In every cycle, some submitted work requires extra scrutiny. Some work may be incomplete, incorrectly formatted, missing parts, suspected of plagiarism, or have any of several other issues. Any work that falls into that category is scored by an additional person, usually a supervisor. With 20,000+ candidates, the number of components needing special attention can be large. These all require extra time to sort through and be deemed compete. It's usually September, October, or maybe even November before these are resolved and finalized. Remember, everyone who scores is an actively working teacher, so the workforce is reduced because most scorers are back in school teaching. Most of the issues at this level are addressed by supervisors.

Scores must be inputted into the system, and a whole series of checks are conducted to assure that each and every score is first, correctly assessed, then entered into the system correctly. Statistical data are run to assure accuracy of every score and input.

All scoring and checking procedures must be complete before any score is released—scores can't be released piecemeal. So it's easily late November into December before every check, every step is complete and ready for release. There is even more to the process than I am aware of because I am not an assessor. It's a comprehensive, complex process, and there is always more than meets the eye.

Although it's hard to wait months for your score, we should all be glad it's so thorough because it ensures the highest degree of accuracy possible—which means that when you get your score, it will be correct. It's not ridiculous that all this takes time. You don't want to be the one whose score is rushed just so you can see it sooner. The process is designed for your benefit. Many professional certifications/licenses take considerable time to process, not just this one. I hope this explanation will help you better understand the scoring process and encourage you to take a deep breath and accept that you'll need to draw on your patience. The wait gives you time and space to find your way back to "normal" and get a positive start to your school year.

Specifics of the Process

No feedback statements are provided for Component 1. Standardized Feedback Statements are provided for Components, 2, 3, and 4 if they receive a score below 3.75. The statements are directly connected to the five Core Propositions AND the NB Standards. They are also connected to particular prompts (which are also connected to the Propositions & Standards) within each component. Your assessment is based on how strongly you show you include the Propositions and Standards in your teaching practice. Language is **nuanced** among levels.

You Can Understand Your Scores

Scores designations encompass four levels numbered from 0 to 4. Each level has information and specific feedback statements to show the level of accomplishment demonstrated within each component. Statements are tailored to the content and rubric statements of each component, so they vary to some degree from component to component. However, all statements, across the components, have a common structure. Here is a general explanation of each level.

Level 0—NOT SCORABLE (NS): This score is the lowest and most serious score designation. Reasons can range from not submitting a component or not attending your assessment center appointment to being suspected of plagiarism. There are a number of other possible reasons for a "0". Refer to the Scoring Guide, page 7 for a more complete list.

Level 1: Level 1 statements begin with the words, ***"You may wish to provide evidence of ___. OR You may wish to focus on ___."*** This means evidence to address/support the prompts is severely lacking or missing altogether. The writing may have gotten seriously off-track. *Evidence* can refer to specific examples/rationales within a prompt response and/or support for the writing in the form of student work samples (C2), video and instructional materials (C3), and KOS/Assessment/ PLN/SN data (C4). It can also indicate that prompts or parts of prompts, forms, or other sections of a component were missing.

Level 2: A "" is the most commonly received score amongst all candidates. Level 2 statements begin with the words: ***"You may wish to provide CLEARER evidence of/that___."*** This means you presented *SOME* evidence, but *MORE* was needed. Likely more specifics and/or rationales were needed. Writing may have been too general. Writing may not be clear or may not have been supported with specifics and/or rationales. There may have been inconsistencies. Evidence submitted might not have been tightly connected to the goals/lessons.

Level 3: Level 3 statements begin with the words: ***"You may wish to provide more CONSISTENT and CONVINCING evidence of ___."*** This means you submitted ample evidence, but may have needed more/stronger specifics and/or rationales. There may have been minor inconsistencies. Note that any score in the 3-family is considered high and accomplished.

Components that receive a 3.75 or higher do not receive any feedback statements. The work is obviously accomplished.

What Works: Notice the **progression/nuance** of language through the levels

Level 1: You may wish to focus on, provide evidence of/that, review instructions to ___.

Level 2: You may wish to provide clearer evidence of/that ___.

Level 3: You may wish to provide more consistent and convincing evidence of ___.

These are clues to help you understand where and how you could do better if you retake a component.

Why This Works

Honing in on the nuances of the wording allows you to analyze and reflect on your previous submission to see where and how it could be strengthened.

What Works

To be fully informed, it is imperative to read the Scoring Guide in its entirety. Every aspect of the scoring process is explained. A comprehensive understanding of the process serves to inform and enhance your work to lead to certification.

8 Confusing Terms, Topics, and FAQs

Six-Word Memoir: Reflecting on teaching brings enlightening insight
ANNIE, NM

What Does Those Terms Mean?

Every year and in every certificate area, candidates seem to struggle with similar sets of challenges within the process. In the spring, Facebook pages that focus on National Board Certification light up with frantic requests for clarification.

Part of the issue stems from the language in the component directions. Prompts are written to give candidates the broadest range of possibilities, which is a double-edged sword. It means both that there are few limitations placed on pedagogy, for example. But the lack of specifics may contribute to difficulty deciphering "what the National Board wants" or "what the assessors expect to see." Some terms used are National Board jargon, so they may not be familiar to all. And finally, the prompts are often long and contain multiple parts within commas and/or parentheses that must be addressed. Here are the top ten topics that candidates bring up again and again, along with *fabricated, abbreviated* examples to clarify each.

1. ***Overarching Goal, Goal(s), Major Idea, Objectives, and Activities:*** Most certificates have one or more prompts that asks you to describe one or more of these elements in your lesson sequence. Not every certificate asks for all of these.
    - *Overarching Goal/Major Idea:* This is the biggest idea, concept, or understanding you want students to take away from the unit of study. It is something that can cut across a variety of areas of a topic and may be difficult to measure. It's often articulated with the word *understand*. Example: The students **will understand** there are a variety of ways to organize and interpret information about people, places, and environments; or, Students **will understand** that writing is a means of communicating with an audience.

- *Goal:* This is another broad understanding of a topic, but slightly more specific than the overarching goal. It is still conceptual; the learning may be difficult to measure and is also often articulated with the word *understand*. *Example: The students **will understand** that maps interpret physical and man-made features.* The verb used in goal statements often comes from one of the higher levels of Bloom's Taxonomy and needs to be more conceptual than concrete.

- *Objective:* The objective describes the specific, measurable learning(s) you want to occur within a particular lesson. *Example: The students **will identify** physical and man-made features on a map.* The verb(s) used in the objective statement may come from one of the lower levels of Bloom's Taxonomy, is relatively concrete, and articulates a student action to be taken. Learning of objectives can be measured/evaluated.

- *Activity:* This is what the students *do* to *learn/practice* the objective. *Example: Students **will construct/draw** a map that includes physical and man-made features.* When the activity is completed, the teacher will be able to assess whether or not students learned the objective. Notice the concrete, active voice verb used to construct the statement.

Be very careful *not* to plan a lesson sequence/unit of study based mainly on activities. It is important for the goals and objectives planned *first*. Plan the activities *last,* otherwise the goal(s) and objective(s) may not be tightly connected.

2. **Instructional Context and Contextual Information:** The very names of these documents guarantee a mix-up. They are like kissing cousins—which is which? They have elements in common but aren't really the same.

    - *Instructional Context (IC)* is about your *class.* This is the first section of your Written Commentary in Component 2 (all certificates), and is a separate form in Components 3 and 4. It gives the assessor a snapshot of your class and your teaching situation (context). Conditions and students you highlight here need to be referenced again in the Written Commentary. While the questions are the same for Instructional Context in Component 2 and on the Forms, your responses may not be identical because either you are addressing a different subject for each or a different aspect of your subject for each. A Literacy candidate is addressing the students taught for Writing, Reading, Speaking, Listening, and Viewing, an MCGen is addressing Writing, and/or Social Studies and Science, and a middle school Math teacher is addressing Mathematical Thinking and Reasoning, Mathematical Discourse, and Small-Group Mathematical Collaborations. For all certificates, the groups used for each component may or may not be the same.

- *Contextual Information (CI):* This form is about your *school* and possibly your district. Here you describe any special programs you teach under, state mandates, type of community your school/district is located in and your access to technology. You need one for *each component* and if your component features students from more than one school, you'll need one for each school. If you have more than one school, Label one as "A" and one as "B" and refer to them that way.

3. **Instructional Materials**: Instructional Materials (IMs) are items used or produced during a teaching sequence. They allow assessors to better understand the activity in your video or Written Commentary. They are not scored separately but are considered a part of your component. They may be submitted in the same form in which they are presented to the class. The National Board FAQ section states that Instructional Materials may be samples of student work unless otherwise specifically stated in the component. Choose Instructional Materials that help the assessor know about the *teaching* you did, the content you covered and/or enrichment or remediation—things that help the assessor to gain a more complete picture of your lesson. Read details in your instructions for submitting computer graphics etc.

4. **Formatting and Editing**: Both of these figure large in producing your final component copies. Page limits demand clear, concise writing, which is always a challenge. You cannot exceed the page limits. At the end of the maximum number of pages allowed, the assessors simply stop reading. It is a good idea to stick as closely as possible to the suggested page limits give for each section of an

component. The National Board knows approximately how much space is needed for well-crafted responses. If you write far less or far more, you are probably either leaving out important evidence or adding fluff.

- *Formatting:* Your portfolio instructions give very specific formatting specifications that must be followed exactly. The basics include using eleven-point Arial font, double-spacing and 1inch margins. But each certificate and each component within certificates have specifications particular to that component. So my best advice is to read and re-read those instructions. There can be issues such as margins that print with 1inch borders on one printer but not another to deal with. My advice is to find a printer that produces the margins you need and use it.
- *Editing:* Most candidates start the writing process by writing everything they can think of; the natural consequence of which is that some serious editing needs to take place. Here are ten tips for editing:
- Use active voice verbs: Eliminate –ing forms and helping verbs; *plan, create.*
- Use "I" in statements with an active verb; *I organized . . . I taught.*
- Indent paragraphs 2 or 3 spaces instead of 5 spaces.
- Use 1 space between sentences/after periods.
- Eliminate "that, the, this, and my" as often as possible. This rarely changes the meaning of a sentence.
- Turn on automatic hyphenation if your program has it. Word has it; Google Docs doesn't.
- Turn off widows and orphans. In your toolbar, find the Paragraph section. Click on the arrow in the bottom right corner. On the new page, click on the Line and page breaks tab and remove the checkmark from widows and orphans.
- Start your text on the same line as a heading; *Instructional Context: The class featured in this component*
- Eliminate adjectives and adverbs where possible.
- See Appendix:10 Editing Tips for even more ideas.

5. **Using *Names/Identification***: As far as possible, use only first names, or some other identifying label such as Student A, Student B, or initials, and so on. Avoid using the name of your state, school, or district. However, if a student calls you by name in a video, that isn't an issue. Always email or call 1-800-22TEACH for specific clarification.
6. **Other *Confusing Terms***: National Board terminology is often different that the everyday terms used by teachers across the country, and that often leads to confusion.
   - *Instructional/Lesson Sequence:* A series of related lessons and/or activities that support a common goal or theme. It is not limited to a single lesson or activity. *Example: A lesson sequence on force and motion.*
   - *Unit:* Part of an academic course focusing on a selected theme or concept. A unit may also refer to a chapter in a curriculum text.
   - *Featured Lesson:* The lesson shown in a video or from which student work samples were derived.
   - *Evidence:* Accomplished teaching *examples* or student *actions* that have a strong foundation in fact, would be convincing to most people, and would not be easily disproved by interpretation. Assessors want to know that you recognized evidence and used them in your teaching. *Example: When he said, I knew that he misunderstood the concept, so I referred him back to the graphic organizer. I knew she had trouble tracking print left to right so I . . .*
   - *Small-group discussion:* Used in a video to show how a teacher facilitates interactions among students. Generally, it is a group of three to five students although group size may vary according to specific component directions.
   - *Whole-class/Large-group lesson:* Used in videos to show the teacher effectively engaging the entire class as a group. There should be evidence of interactions with individual students but not necessarily every student. However it should be clear that the whole class is actively engaged in the lesson.

National Board Certification Is Rigorous Professional Development

National Board Certification is meant to be a rigorous process that takes deep thinking and broad knowledge to accomplish. Every certificate has particular challenges, but the entire process challenges teachers to formulate effective learning *for these students, at this time, in this setting,* to promote rigorous professional development in the highest form.

9 Candidate Care

You know you are a National Board Candidate if you can write your components anywhere: in the car, during TV commercials, in the faculty room, in church, or even in the bathroom.

Taking Care of Yourself

If you are reading this at the beginning of your candidacy, you may wonder why there is a chapter devoted to this topic. If you are well into your candidacy or near the end, you may now recognize the need to take care of yourself and wish you had realized or admitted it sooner. Going through the National Board Certification process is labor-intensive, time-consuming, and brain-challenging—all factors that can take a toll on your mental and physical well-being. But no matter where you are in the process, it's never too late to take care of yourself.

Gain the Gift of Time—*Just For Now*

Doing some groundwork early in your candidacy can save much stress and frustration later. Your most precious resource will be *time*: time to think, time to plan, time to write.

What Works! Here are the top four ideas that can ferret out the valuable time you'll need:

1. *Ask for support from your family.*
   - *Just for now*, delegate some jobs you've always done yourself. Can the kids fold the laundry and change their own beds? Can your spouse regularly take the kids on an outing during a weekend afternoon so you can have an uninterrupted block of writing time? Can someone other than you be responsible for keeping the house picked-up? Can you assign each person one room? Could your spouse help with the grocery shopping once a week or bathe the baby?

2. *Ask for support at school.*
   - *Just for now,* ask your principal to let you off the hook for serving on major committees. Most candidates are active members of their school community and often take leadership roles that are time-consuming. Attending frequent school meetings will eat away at the time you need for planning and writing your components. Explain that you will need many hours beyond the school day to work on your components and that being excused from committees *just for now* would be an amazing help. Promise to come back next year as soon as you're finished!
   - Ask your principal/district for one teacher workday/sub day during second semester for each component you plan to submit.
3. *Find a National Board support group, cohort, or buddy.*
   - *Just for now, make meeting with other candidates a priority.*
   - Join a support group and attend regularly if such cohorts are offered in your district. You'll have an NBCT facilitator who can guide you through the process, and you'll meet other candidates you can work with, share with, and sympathize with. And they can do the same for you . . . it's a "you scratch my back and I'll scratch yours" kind of symbiotic arrangement that is mutually beneficial.
   - Look at surrounding districts if there is no formal cohort in your district. I've never heard of a cohort that turned down someone who wanted to participate. Most groups meet monthly, so even if it involves a drive, it will likely be worth the effort.
   - Find a buddy—a fellow candidate in your district or one who lives near enough to meet with periodically. To find one, look up National Board Certification in your state and ask for a list of candidates. Plan to meet both online frequently and in person at least monthly during the first semester and more often as the deadline nears.
   - Join one or more National Board Facebook pages that serve as forums for all certificate areas. There are also certificate-specific groups, but not all specialized groups are as active as pages serving all certificate areas. Just a word of *caution: never send your actual work to someone you don't know!* If someone plagiarizes your work, there could be negative consequences for both you and the plagiarizer. Suggested Facebook pages:

- National Board Certified Teacher—I am an administrator on this page.
- National Board Certified Teacher on Facebook—I am an administrator on this page.
- NBCT Support
- Exceptional Needs—NBCTs and Candidates
- National Board Certification Survival Group
- FB groups for English Teachers, MCGens, ECGens, Science, Social Studies/History, CTE, Music, Mathematics, and School Counseling

4. *Find a weekend or period when you can have uninterrupted work time.*
   - *Just once,* plan to give yourself a working retreat—especially in the spring. If someone you know has a cabin or beach house, ask if you can use it. Rent a room at a hotel. Send your family out of town for a weekend so you can have the house to yourself. Be creative to find a way to carve out some extra precious time. Sometimes this can work with a buddy, but only if you can limit conversation and concentrate on YOUR needs.

Why These Work! These strategies are proven to boost your efficiency, give you the gift of time, and give you the support and resources you'll need.

Procrastination: Your Worst Enemy

Procrastination is seriously the worst judgment error you can make as a National Board Candidate—*seriously!* It will do you in faster than most people can lick an ice-cream cone on a summer day. Many believe that they do their best work under pressure. This may actually be true for one or two out of a hundred candidates. But the other ninety-eight who think they work best under pressure are almost always mistaken; at least in this case. Writing a National Board component is time intensive and cannot be accomplished by pulling an all-nighter—or even two or three. Candidates who score well have usually devoted weeks if not months to planning and writing a component. They plan and video multiple lessons. They write and revise components multiple times.

As an NBCT who has facilitated hundreds of candidates, I can tell you firsthand that procrastination is a devastating habit. It would take more than two hands to count the number of candidates I've seen who put off reading their standards, put off reading the portfolio instructions, put off planning lessons that met the component requirements, put off collecting student work samples, put off filming lessons, and put off writing. I've had candidates who let it slip in March that they hadn't yet read their directions or made a single video. Most of those candidates did not certify on their first attempt. There is just no way to produce the quality portfolio the National Board expects if one repeatedly and consistently procrastinates.

The fact that I've devoted nearly a full page of text to procrastination should tell you how seriously I regard this as a fatal flaw. You can be Teacher of the Year, be the best teacher at your school, but if you don't devote the time and energy to planning and writing, your chances of certifying are slim .There are many reasons teachers don't certify on their first attempt, but please don't let *procrastination* be the reason *you* don't certify. It is an avoidable pitfall.

What Works! Activate! Don't Procrastinate! Procrastination is inaction. The best thing you can do is to take action. Taking action has many benefits that will serve you well as you work through the process, and it might just save you at the end.

Being Proactive

What does being a proactive National Board Candidate mean? It means you don't worry and stew for weeks or months before actually *doing the* things that need to be done. Consider:

- Read your Standards *often* and *really well*. Highlight the examples given in each one to refer to later. NBCTs always tell candidates to read their Standards thoroughly and often and there is a reason for that. You have to know them and show them to certify.
- Read your component instructions *really well*. You can't produce lessons that will score well unless you truly know what the component asks you to do. Ninety-nine percent of what you need to know and do is in your instructions. Period! Get intimate with the instructions!
- Get started on *something*. Chunk out the work. Find one thing in a component to start working on soon. Once you get the ball rolling,

it's more likely you'll keep going. The Instructional Context part of the Written Commentary or Forms can be good starting places. Or respond to one prompt—do anything to get started.
- Get a system in place to organize your components and materials. Being able to lay your hands on something when you need it will be an enormous help as you go along.
- Set aside a designated work time each week. Stick to it and use it.

Why These Work! Proactive behaviors will keep you on track, raise your confidence level, and produce results that will pay off. Think of yourself as being a sculptor chipping away little by little at the marble slab. Eventually the sculptor's chipping brings into being a beautiful statue. By chipping away steadily section by section, prompt by prompt, form by form, you will produce a fully formed, thoughtful portfolio that documents your accomplished teaching.

Paying Attention to Your Health

As I mentioned in this chapter's opening paragraph, the National Board Certification process is labor-intensive, time-consuming, and brain challenging. All of these things take a toll on the body, mind and spirit especially during the last three months. But there are things you can do to minimize the effects all this hard work can heap on you.

Your Body

- Eat right and stay hydrated. I know . . . yada, yada, yada. You hear this all the time. But considering that you may be doing more sitting than usual at the computer, keeping the carbs, and sugar consumption under control could make a difference in the way you feel. You've heard of the "Freshman Fifteen" pounds college freshmen gain during their first year away from home? Try to avoid the "National Board Nine." It's no fun trying to lose weight! Keep a bottle or glass of water handy at the computer and drink it!
- Exercise—take some walks. Again, yada, yada, yada . . . but this is another thing that can make a difference. Fit in some short walks—alone if possible. Walking seems to get the juices flowing . . . to your

muscles and your brain. I practically wrote some components in my head while on walks. I seemed to be able to think more clearly and figure out how to get past blocks I was experiencing. Outdoor walks worked best for me when the weather permitted . . . maybe the noise at the gym competed with the "noise" in my head. And sometimes I didn't want the hassle of going to the gym. Just heading out my door and walking through the neighborhood worked for me.

- Exercise at your computer. As you get into writing your components, you'll spend hours sitting and typing. Learn some chair exercises and stretches you can do every thirty minutes or so to stretch your neck, shoulder, arm, and wrist muscles. They take so little time yet feel so good and will help prevent a lot of aches and pains. Google "chair exercises" and get lots of choices. Stand up at least every half-hour.
  - Do some yoga stretches/poses when you need a break. Yoga is quiet, calm and gentle, and energizing. You will feel so much better, I guarantee.

Your Mind

All of the above will help your state of mind, but try these as well.

- Positive self-talk can work wonders. To combat those feelings that you are going crazy, that you are overwhelmed, that this is too hard, formulate some positive statements to help you relax. Try incorporating these thoughts into your mindset:
  - *I can figure this out.*
  - *I'm doing my best.*
  - *I'll come back to this later.*
  - *I'll answer just one prompt now.*
  - *I know how to do this.*
  - *This is a common feeling for candidates to have.*
  - *I'm not alone in this process.*
  - *Slow down and approach one prompt/section at a time.*
  - *I'll read the directions one more time.*
  - *I'll read this standard again.*
  - *I'll make a list.*

- *I'll ask my buddy, mentor, cohort, or website for support.*
- *I can adjust my schedule just for today/this week/until this entry is done.*

Your Spirit

Taking care of your physical and mental needs will automatically lift your spirits. As you encounter obstacles, you'll find yourself more resilient and able to rebound. You can recognize that tackling a difficult challenge always involves setbacks and frustrations, but you won't let them derail your efforts. You'll be able to continue on in a more positive frame of mind.

What Works!

Planning to care for yourself will help you have the energy you need. You'll have the confidence, stamina, and perseverance to see the challenge through to the end.

Why These Work!

Your body will find a way to take a break one way or another. It's much better for YOU to plan the breaks your body will take rather than find yourself ill and unable to work. As a teacher, you are already exposed to massive doses of germs from your students, so do all you can to keep yourself healthy—in body, mind, and spirit!

Appendix A
Ten Commandments for Survival as a National Board Candidate

THOU SHALT:

I. Read Thy Directions and Pay Attention to All Details Contained Therein! Know formatting requirements and page requirements.

II. Make Thy Videos Early! When you signed on for this gig, you didn't realize you'd need to become an overnight "Steven Spielberg." Plan your videos to show the elements the assessors are looking for.

III. Thou Shalt Not Procrastinate! Work steadily and don't put off until tomorrow what you can do today. Procrastination is your worst enemy in this process.

IV. Thou Shalt Save Everything! Promise yourself that you will never turn off your computer without backing up and dating all of your work.

V. Learn that Verbs are Thy Friends! Use the active voice and analytical and reflective verbs that will help you respond to the prompts.

VI. Learn that Adjectives and Fluff are Thy Enemies! These are space-hogs and don't add evidence. Stick to a spare, text-book style writing style.

VII. Seek Out Others to Critique Thy Components and Bruise Thy Ego Because They Will Heal Thy Writing! Ask others to read your entries to be sure your writing is clear, consistent, and convincing. Getting feedback can lead to better scores.

VIII. Complete your Electronic Submission Before the Deadline Date! Uploading and submitting take longer than you might imagine, so allow plenty of time!

IX. Prepare for Component 1 as Soon as Thou Submits Other Components! Heave a sigh of relief at finishing your portfolio, then get ready to demonstrate your content knowledge by reviewing content that spans the age range of your certificate.

X. Bask in the knowledge that Thou Art Among the Minority of Teachers Who Attempt National Board Certification! You have completed a remarkable journey that fewer than 10 percent of all teachers even attempt, let alone finish. Give thyself a well-deserved pat on the back!

Appendix B
Ten Editing Tips to Trim Space without Trimming Content

1. Turn OFF "widow/orphan" control if your program has it. This prevents a single line of a paragraph from being at the top of a new page. You'll save several lines in the space of an entry.
2. Turn ON auto-hyphenate if your program has it. This will break words at the ends of lines to properly hyphenate. Saving even a few spaces on each page can help.
3. Use contractions. They save several spaces each time you use them. Word has an auto-correct feature called "Find and Replace." You may need to do this for each contraction.
4. Use numerals such as 12 instead of twelve and 6th instead of sixth. You can break the rule you learned in school. EXAMPLE: Video Analysis: "This lesson features 89 1st graders learning to sharpen pencils."
5. Make sure your header with the Candidate # is outside the margin and not in the body.
6. Find and replace the period-double-space. This is another space saver.
7. Take *the, my, this, and that* out of most sentences. The meaning won't change but you'll gain space. Replace: *I collected the papers* with *I collected papers*. *I know that students . . .* with *I know students . . .*
8. Remove as many adjectives and adverbs as possible: Replace: *She writes with vivid and inspired word choice* . . . . . . with *She writes with strong word choice*
9. Indent paragraphs 2 or 3 spaces instead of 5, *or* eliminate paragraphs altogether. If you choose the latter, **bold** or <u>underline</u> the first word or two as a visual aid to the assessor.

Appendix C
Sentence Stems for Analytic and Reflective Writing

- I chose ___ because ___.
- The rationale behind my decision was ___.
- Because I know ___, I ___.
- The __ on his paper showed me ___, so I ___.
- First I ___, then I followed up by ___.
- This was significant because ___.
- When I saw ___, I realized ___.
- In order to ___, I ___.
- The reasons I chose ___ were ___.
- I used a variety of strategies including ___, ___, and ___.
- I saw the error was caused by ___, so I ___.
- As a result of ___, Jennifer was able to ___.

Appendix D
Component 3: Analysis of a Video

Table D.1 Topic / Lesson

Minute	Teacher Talk	Student Talk	Interaction S/S S/T T/S	Evidence of Prompt/ Rubric Bullet
1:00				
2:00				
3:00				
4:00				
5:00				
6:00				
7:00				
9:00				
10:00				
11:00				
12:00				
13:00				
14:00				
15:00				
			Students to student	
			Students to teacher	
			Teacher to student	

Appendix E
Video Tips for Component 3

Below are some tips for analyzing the Component 3 videos. Candidates respond to the same prompts twice—once for each video.

Candidates need to understand:

- Each video shows a separate lesson.
- Each video highlights a different instructional format (whole/large group; small group/other). More than one format can be evident on a single video, but ONE must be clearly dominant.
- Each video must capture evidence of your teaching practice (instruction), learning environment, and student engagement.

When analyzing a video, look for these elements:

- In the "Selecting a Video" section (pages 7 & 8 in most certificate directions) are a set of bullets addressing the areas of learning environment, student engagement, and instruction.
- Find as many examples of these bullet points as possible—both in the video(s) and in the writing. Some will be overt: words spoken, questions asked, room arrangement, resources, on-topic, academic discussion, etc. Others will be more subtle: tone of voice, body language/eye contact, on task behaviors, etc.
- The more examples found, the better. Points not visible in the video(s), but evident in the lesson, should be referenced in the writing.
- Two prompts in the Written Commentary directly ask candidates to cite evidence from the video. The video segment chosen MUST show those examples.

Important Questions:

- What is the goal of the lesson?
- What instructional format(s) is shown on the video(s)?
- What examples of each bullet point are evident in the video(s)?
- What evidence/examples can you cite from the video(s) as responses to the prompts that ask directly for examples from the video(s)?

Appendix F
SSTARS Lesson Plan Template Based on the Architecture of Accomplished Teaching

Table F.1 Lesson Plan Template

STUDENTS (Step 1: Knowledge of Students) **WHAT I KNOW ABOUT:** • These students at this time, **in this setting** • Learning styles • Abilities • Needs • Prior Knowledge	
SET GOALS (Step 2: Set high, worthwhile goals) • Goals • Objectives • Activities • Unifying Concepts/Big Ideas	
TEACH (Step 3: Implement instruction) • Appropriate strategies • Activities support goals • Appropriate pacing	
ASSESS (Step 4: Evaluate learning in light of the goals) • Monitor progress purposefully • Assess throughout the lesson sequence • Observations • Informal • Formal • Remediate/Enrich	
REFLECT (Step 5: Reflect on student learning) • Effectiveness • Successes • Modification	
START AGAIN (Step 6: Set new high, worthwhile goals) • For these students, at this time, in this setting	

Appendix G
Twenty Tips from Component 4 Assessors

1. NEVER shrink/reduce evidence. It must be readable at 100 percent magnification.
2. Follow YOUR certificate's instructions regarding the PROFILE GROUP size and makeup. Most certificates require a WHOLE CLASS.
3. Dig deep into the Knowledge of Students (KOS). Go beyond demographics. Your KOS NB Standard has many ideas.
4. Give specific data. If you say you collected data from a source, specifically describe that data and what you learned about your students from that data.
5. Know the NB definitions and purposes of Formative, Summative, and Student Self-Assessments. Particularly be aware of the *timing* of each within the component. Read the Portfolio Related Terms in the GENERAL Portfolio Instructions.
6. Be sure to address the IMPACT on student learning of your Professional Learning Need and in the Student Need. Use evidence that backs up your claims of impact.
7. Follow the page counts within the files you submit—don't go over! Do not alter forms in any way.
8. Choose a PLN and SN that have been fully implemented—otherwise it's not a good choice.
9. If your PLN and SN are related to each other, you cannot use the same evidence for both. The PLN is about your LEARNING. The SN is about COLLABORATION, etc. The evidence must match the need.
10. Strong PLN evidence goes beyond a PD certificate. Choose evidence that shows notes, agendas, or other data that shows YOUR learning.
11. Begin planning and collecting evidence for the PLN and SN early in the year so you have time to implement your plans and gather data.

12. The PLN and SN are about GROUPS, not individuals. If you teach ONLY 1:1, state that in your writing/on the forms.
13. Email evidence should have substance about the need—beyond "Let's meet." or "Thanks for the meeting." For example, a SN email might address collaboration or advocacy & its impact.
14. Do not waste character space listing the Standards or using phrases such as *As an accomplished teacher, I___*. Use your space for specific evidence and rationales.
15. Submit only one version of the FA or SA—do not submit multiple versions. You can briefly explain if you used different versions. It's okay to submit different forms of the Student Self-Assessment.
16. The PLN and/or the SN CAN be about your Profile Group or can be about a different group.
17. Although it's not a hard and fast rule, answering the prompts in the order given is most helpful to the assessors. This writing is not a narrative telling a story.
18. Answer the prompts on forms with specificity
19. Check formatting: double space the Written Commentary. It's okay to have a page of evidence in landscape format (assessors can flip them), but use portrait for all other writing.
20. FOLLOW DIRECTIONS, FOLLOW DIRECTIONS!

About the Author

Bobbie Faulkner spent thirty-eight years teaching grades K-6 in Kentucky, Ohio, and Arizona. She is a middle childhood generalist who was originally certified in 1999 and renewed her National Board Certificate in 2008. She has been a Candidate Support Provider for more than a decade and has mentored hundreds of candidates in person and through online websites. She's written four previous What Works! series books both for the former versions and a Components 1 and 2 update for Version 3.0.